The Flat Earth Bible

A Detailed Explanation of Biblical Flat Earth

Written by: Kenny Williamson

Website: kennywilliamson.com

First Edition

Paperback Edition

ISBN: 979-8345545515

1Co 3:19 For the wisdom of this world is foolishness with God. For it is written, He taketh the wise in their own craftiness.

Table of Contents

Forward

In The Flat Earth Bible, Kenny offers a compelling look at the Bible's clear support for a flat, geocentric Earth. This book is a journey of faith, discovery, and courage. Kenny once accepted the heliocentric model of the universe without question, as we all had, until he took a closer look at the Bible. With fresh eyes, he began to see verses he had read countless times in a new light—verses that revealed a flat, stationary Earth under a firmament.

Kenny lays out a thoughtful, verse-by-verse argument, challenging us to break free from the assumptions we've been taught since childhood. He points out that science, media, and space agencies like NASA have outright lied to us, leading us astray and replacing God's creation with a man-made version that contradicts scripture. This book isn't just about Flat Earth; it's about a world that has lost its spiritual center and an invitation to return to the truth of God's Word.

If you're a Bible believer willing to question everything, you'll find The Flat Earth Bible both enlightening and encouraging. Kenny's journey should just inspire you to look at the world and the heavens through a biblical and actual scientific lens.

Flat Earth Dave

Preface

Hello, my name is Kenny Williamson, and I am a born-again Christian and a Bible believer. For most of my life, I believed in a heliocentric model of the universe, which consisted of a globe-shaped Earth along with other planets orbiting around the Sun. This is what I was taught in school, and I assumed it to be true. I did not fully understand how it all worked, and I never trusted the so-called scientist to know either. I just figured that God created it all and was holding it all together. I knew that most of the scientists were godless evolutionists, and they were guessing at theories on how the universe came into existence based on heathenistic views, all while denying the Biblical story of creation.

I have now concluded that we are not living on a heliocentric model but a geocentric one, otherwise known as Flat Earth. I had heard of a Flat Earth in the past and immediately dismissed it as a fallacy. It was not until recently, in 2024, that I was reintroduced to the Flat Earth model again. Initially, I rejected it as I had always done, but this time, something kept telling me to dig a little deeper. As I began to do my research, I found that there were many references to a geocentric model of Earth in the Bible. It was there the whole time, staring me right in the face. I had read most of these verses many times, but they had never clicked. This time, when I reread the verses, I realized what I had missed.

These verses were always there, but I was reading them with a satanic heliocentric veil over my eyes. I was reading these verses with the preconceived idea that the Earth was out in a never-ending vacuum of space. There is a stark difference when comparing these verses with what you are indoctrinated with in public schools. However, I was justifying my belief in the heliocentric model by assuming that God's word meant something other than what it actually said. I was trying to apply man's so-called science to the Bible when I should have been measuring the science against what the Bible says is true. When you begin to put God's word first, the man-made satanic science falls apart.

I also believe that the Bible is a book that is to be taken literally. Too many so-called Christians today try to spiritualize everything in the Bible and manage to twist it into whatever they want it to say. I could write volumes on what the Bible says and what people think it says, but that is a topic for another book. In this book, I will try to focus on what the Bible says about a Flat Earth. Most of the information that I will present to you here is easy to understand; it's just hard to believe.

What makes some of these verses hard to believe is the fact that most of the population today has been indoctrinated since birth to believe in the heliocentric model of theEarth. We have been indoctrinated by Hollywood since the 1950s with movies about space travel and rockets to Mars. Nearly everything produced by Hollywood promotes either aliens from outer space, distant planets in space, the Earth being a planet in space, or, most recently, colonizing Mars. I have always been a science fiction fan, and I have always enjoyed watching space movies. However, once you mature in Christ, you need to open your eyes and realize that Hollywood is a satanic movie-making organization designed to keep you confused and depressed. Its primary function is to keep you from ever getting saved. You need to remember that as the lyrics to a popular song go, "Space may be the final frontier, but it's made in a Hollywood basement."

Hollywood, coupled with our own satanic government, has been promoting the heliocentric model of the Earth since the late 1950s. NASA, as we know it, got its start in 1958 and used Nazi scientists to further its agenda. I have been asked several times why they would lie. Well, that is a good question, and I believe it has a couple of different answers, which are explained in detail in this book.

Just like the Bible, this book is not a science book. However, there are some scientific facts listed. There are several sites that you can view that pertain to Flat Earth, and I will list some at the back of the book. I believe that this is a spiritual battle between good and evil. I hope you keep an open mind while reading this book and try to go and verify anything that I have said for yourself.

In the first part of this book, I have included chapters to help you understand some of what is being taught versus what is the truth. Please read them with an open mind and then compare them to what the Bible has to say. I personally don't care what the scientists say; I believe the Bible. I am new to the Flat Earth thing, and I don't have all the answers. There are many questions that I still have, and I am still looking for the answers. I hope this book helps you to get your foot in the door and encourages you to do your own research.

One of my main goals with this book was to make it simple and easy to read. In doing so, there is lots of technical data on these different subjects that I did not include. This data is available on many sites that you can research for yourself. I wanted this book to be a go-to handbook for any of your questions. I tried to write each chapter so you don't have to read them in any particular order. Just pick a topic and read about it.

I have heard many times that once you discover the Flat Earth truth, you can never go back to the globe; you will have to see for yourself. I pray that no matter what you believe about the shape of the Earth, you find salvation in Jesus Christ. Good luck in your journey, and Godspeed.   *Kenny*

Why Would They Lie?

To fully understand the answers to this question, we have to cover some biblical ground. I will try to explain this as briefly and simply as possible while still providing a good explanation. The very first thing you have to understand is that Satan is the god of this world. Satan was given free reign here, and he is referred to as the prince of the power of the air.

Eph 2:2 Wherein in time past ye walked according to the course of this world, according to the prince of the power of the air, the spirit that now worketh in the children of disobedience:

Satan is in full control over everything on this Earth. Satan was removed from heaven because of his pride and wanting to take God's place. Satan now hates God. Satan also hates mankind because God loves us.

Eze 28:17 Thine heart was lifted up because of thy beauty, thou hast corrupted thy wisdom by reason of thy brightness: I will cast thee to the ground, I will lay thee before kings, that they may behold thee.

Now, seeing how Satan hates mankind, it is one of his main goals to keep man from getting saved. Satan is also a liar and the father of lies.

Joh 8:44 Ye are of your father the devil, and the lusts of your father ye will do. He was a murderer from the beginning, and abode not in the truth, because there is no truth in him. When he speaketh a lie, he speaketh of his own: for he is a liar, and the father of it.

With this knowledge, it is very easy to piece together what is happening and why. Satan is in control of this Earth. Satan hates God, and he hates Mankind. Satan is a liar. Everything that God does, Satan tries to copy and destroy. Satan does not want mankind to believe in God or to get saved. Satan is very smart and cunning. What he does is he takes everything that the Bible teaches and tries to pervert it. He is the opposite of God.

So, If the Bible says that God created the Earth and all of the stars, then Satan says that God did not create it; it was created by an accident, a Big Bang. The Bible says that the Earth is God's footstool, and it is the center of his creation. Satan says that the Earth is not the center of anything but just an insignificant planet out in space, one of trillions. God said that he created the Earth and placed a firmament around it to keep out the waters of the deep. Satan says there is no firmament, and we are surrounded by the vacuum of space. The Bible says that the Sun and Moon move around the Earth in their own circuits. Satan says that the Earth moves around the Sun.

The Bible describes the Earth as being flat, so Satan shows you fake CGI pictures and claims that it is a globe.

This same method is used over and over by Satan to keep you from believing in God and believing that you are a creation of God. Satan is using Hollywood and government agencies like NASA to accomplish this and to keep a steady stream of lies and propaganda in front of your eyes at all times. Satan knows that if you knew the truth about the firmament and how the luminaries you see at night all revolve around the Earth, you would have to come to the conclusion that there is a God, the creator of this Earth.

The other reason that they would lie to the populace about all of this is that the governments of the Earth all want to be in control of you. They all want you to do what they say. If you knew the truth, it would be very hard for the government to control you and your thoughts. Currently, the government uses every kind of scare tactic they can devise to control how you think and what you do.

One of the newest satanic lies that is being pushed is the possibility of an alien invasion from outer space. All you hear about now on the fake news is how an unidentified aerial phenomenon of some kind has been seen. When you know that space, as NASA describes it, is fake, and there is a firmament above the Earth, it becomes apparent that anything they say about space aliens is also fake. If there really is something flying around, they have to be from right here on Earth. They are either from our own government, demonic in nature, or a hologram right out of Project Blue Beam. When you have figured this out, you will not be scared of any of the lies that our government uses to try to control you.

It is also speculated that there are other lands far beyond the Antarctic ice wall. If this is true, the government most likely is hiding lots of resources, all while claiming that our resources here on Earth are drying up. It would seem logical that if this were true, one could simply fly over the southern ice wall and see for themselves. However, due to the Antarctic treaty, travel beyond the area south of 60 degrees South Latitude is prohibited. This treaty was enacted in 1959, right after the formation of NASA. As you will see, they seem to have been very busy in the late 1950s.

Kenny Williamson

NASA's Beginnings

NASA was founded in response to the supposed Soviet Union's launch of Sputnik 1, the world's first artificial satellite, on October 4, 1957. I believe that this so-called satellite was all a hoax. This event marked the beginning of the space race and created concern in the United States about Soviet advancements in space and missile technology. In response, U.S. policymakers decided to prioritize the development of American space exploration programs. They also decided to bilk the taxpayers out of billions of dollars.

The main scientist who played a central role in the early days of NASA in 1958 was Wernher von Braun. Von Braun was a German aerospace engineer and rocket scientist who led the development of the Saturn V rocket that allegedly propelled the Apollo missions to the Moon. I, as well as many others, believe that the Moon landing is also a giant hoax. Before joining NASA, he had worked on rocket technology in Germany for the Nazis during World War II, but he and many of his team were brought to the U.S. under Operation Paperclip after the war.

As NASA formed, von Braun became the main figure in its rocketry and space exploration programs. He led the development of the Red stone and Jupiter rockets and then the Saturn V, which were crucial for NASA's fake Mercury, Gemini, and Apollo programs.

Before von Braun died, he was reported to have said the following to his secretary, Carol Rosin:

'And remember Carol, the last card is the alien card. We're going to have to build space-based weapons against aliens.' And all of it, he said, is a lie."

Also, on von Brauns's headstone, he has the following verse:

Psalm 19:1 The heavens declare the glory of God; and the firmament sheweth his handywork.

Was he trying to tell us something that he knew? He would have known that the Earth is surrounded by a firmament and there is no getting through it. He had to have known that his rockets were going nowhere except out to sea, where they were ditched and then recovered. There are many videos that can be seen of these rockets seeming to be going nowhere. Are these rockets really just shooting out to sea? Are they being ditched in the Bermuda Triangle? Is it a coincidence that the only island in the area, Bermuda Island, is controlled by NASA? The first notable mention of the Bermuda Triangle having to do with mysterious disappearances was also, you guessed it, in the 1950s. Is there a possibility that this entire Bermuda

Triangle thing was nothing more than a rouse to keep people away from that area? Maybe NASA didn't want people out in that area finding their rockets floating around that were supposed to be in "outer space."

On a side note, all of these NASA programs are named after pagan gods and led by Nazi scientists. Just in case you thought that NASA had anything to do with Christ. NASAs main goal is to push the Big Bang theory, Evolution, and to deny that God is the creator. You cannot trust anything that NASA has ever said, for they are doing the devil's work.

Also, in case you missed it, all state-run schools are nothing more than propaganda centers designed to indoctrinate your children. The theory of evolution is taught as a fact to children because it is the state religion. Even though this teaching has been proven to be falsified on every level, they still teach it to children as fact. This is the same for anything that NASA says. It is clearly all lies but taught as truth.

"Planets" are Named after

Pagan gods

The "planets" in our "solar system" are named after figures from ancient mythology, particularly from Roman and Greek mythology. Is that a surprise? Here's a list of the planets and their origins:

Mercury: Named after the Roman messenger god, Mercury, who was associated with speed and communication.

Venus: Named after the Roman goddess of love and beauty, Venus. The planet is often associated with the Greek goddess Aphrodite.

Earth: Meaning "ground" or "soil." It is the only planet not named after a mythological figure. That is because God called it Earth. Even the satanic devils that made up the other names had to stick with what God said.

Mars: Named after the Roman god of war, Mars. The planet's supposedly reddish appearance has often been associated with blood and warfare.

Jupiter: Named after the king of the Roman gods, Jupiter. He is equivalent to the Greek god Zeus.

Saturn: Named after the Roman god of agriculture and time, Saturn. He is also associated with the Greek god Cronus.

Uranus: Named after the ancient Greek deity of the sky, Uranus. It is one of the few planets named directly after a figure from Greek mythology.

Neptune: Named after the Roman god of the sea, Neptune. This name supposedly reflects the planet's deep blue color.

Pluto (now classified as a dwarf planet): Named after the Roman god of the underworld, Pluto. The name was chosen partly because of the planet's distance from the Sun and its cold, dark characteristics.

As you can see, all of these luminaries that NASA refers to as planets were named after pagan gods. The reason for this is a simple one. NASA is a satanic institution designed to deceive the populace and keep you from knowing the truth. Earth is the only one that was named by God himself when he created it. It is the only name that is not somehow connected to the devil.

Is the Bible a Science Book?

The simple answer is no; however, the Bible is never wrong.
I believe now that in order to understand the Bible, you must first be saved. Once you are saved, you are given discernment, and only then can you understand what you are reading. The other thing about the Bible is while it is not a science book, anything written in the Bible about science is true. This is one example of how it took modern science thousands of years to catch up with the Bible. In this particular instance, modern science was not smart enough to figure out that you need to wash your dirty hands. The Bible tells you why you need to wash your hands in Leviticus and several other verses.

Lev 15:13 And when he that hath an issue is cleansed of his issue; then he shall number to himself seven days for his cleansing, and wash his clothes, and bathe his flesh in running water, and shall be clean.

This seems like common sense now, but it took our modern-day doctors and scientists several thousand years to figure this simple thing out. Doctors began to realize the importance of hand-washing in the mid-19th century. The turning point came with the work of Ignaz Semmelweis, a Hungarian physician. In 1847, while working in a Vienna hospital, Semmelweis observed a high rate of infections and maternal deaths in the maternity ward. He noted that doctors were often moving between handling cadavers during autopsies and delivering babies without washing their hands. Real smart, huh?

To test his theory that doctors were inadvertently transmitting infections, Semmelweis instituted a hand-washing policy, requiring doctors to wash their hands with a chlorinated lime solution before interacting with patients. The results were striking—mortality rates in the maternity ward dropped dramatically.

Despite this success, Semmelweis' findings were not widely accepted in his time. His ideas faced resistance from the medical community, who were skeptical of the link between hand hygiene and infection. Semmelweis was eventually dismissed from his position due to his controversial promotion of hand-washing. Fired for hand washing, but this is like science today, disregarding what the Bible teaches.

So there you have a prime example of the Bible telling you to wash your hands and our so-called doctors running several thousand years behind what the Bible teaches. So again, the Bible is not a science book, but whatever science is in the Bible is always true.

What is Flat Earth?

The scientific name for the Flat Earth model is often referred to as the geocentric Flat Earth model or simply the Flat Earth theory. In this model, Earth is conceptualized as a flat plane, with the Sun, Moon, and stars moving above it, often within or beneath a "firmament" or dome. Flat Earth theories often argue that Biblical proofs, visual evidence, and common sense suggest a stationary and flat surface rather than a sphere. I believe that the Bible is filled with many verses that prove Flat Earth.

On the other hand, the scientific name for the globe model is the heliocentric model (from "helios," the Greek word for "Sun"), which suggests that the Earth and other planets orbit around the Sun. This is a satanic form of Sun worship. This fictitious model is widely accepted and taught in modern science and is supported by erroneous data, including CGI imagery, fake astronomical measurements, and so-called laws of gravity and motion formulated by pseudo-scientists like Isaac Newton and Johannes Kepler.

The differences in these two different models are significant. In the heliocentric model, the Earth is a sphere, rotating around its axis and revolving around the Sun.

In the geocentric model or the Flat Earth model, the Earth is a flat plane, often imagined as circular, with edges sometimes surrounded by an "ice wall." This ice wall is also called the Antarctic Basin.

In the heliocentric model, the Earth is one planet among others in orbit around the Sun, which is one of billions of stars in the universe. This, of course, was supposedly all created by chance in the "big bang."

 In the geocentric model, the Earth is stationary, with celestial bodies (Sun, Moon, stars) moving above or within a dome-like firmament. This is all taking place in the vastness of the great deep, not the vastness of outer space. In this model, space, as NASA teaches, is fantasy. There are many references to the Earth's creation and its location in the Bible.

In the heliocentric model, the Earth rotates on its axis at one thousand miles per hour and orbits the Sun at 66,600 miles per hour, while the Moon orbits Earth. They claim the Moon is tidally locked to the Earth, so we only see one side of it.

In the geocentric model, the Sun, Moon, and stars move in circuits above the stationary flat plane of Earth. This is clearly evident by the position of the stars over the last four thousand years of recorded history. These stars have been seen, mapped, and recorded since the beginning of time. If our solar system is moving through an ever-expanding galaxy at over half a million miles per hour, how is it that stars like Polaris never move? Everything that our so-called scientists teach goes against common sense.

In the heliocentric model, "gravity" is an imaginary force that attracts objects towards Earth's center, explaining why objects fall and why planets orbit the Sun. This imaginary force is so strong that it can hold ships upside down on the ocean on the bottom side of the Earth but weak enough to allow birds to fly off that ship. This imaginary force is also able to hold the air to the Earth right next to the perfect vacuum of space. This, of course, goes against all known laws of thermodynamics. But who needs laws anyway?

In the geocentric model, gravity is disputed as traditionally explained, attributing the downward force to other mechanisms (e.g., density and buoyancy). The more dense the object, the more downward force it creates.

Kenny Williamson

Laws of Thermodynamics

According to the second law of thermodynamics, you cannot have a high-pressure system next to a vacuum without separation, such as a physical barrier, because gases naturally move from areas of higher pressure to areas of lower pressure. This is a process known as entropy, where systems equalize in a short amount of time. Essentially, high-pressure gas particles would rapidly expand into the vacuum of space to equalize the pressure difference, as systems in nature spontaneously shift from ordered (high pressure vs. vacuum) to disordered (equilibrium). For some reason, when it comes to NASA, this law does not apply to the Earth and space due to a magical force called gravity.

The first law of thermodynamics also comes into play, which states that energy cannot be created or destroyed but only transferred. When gases move from high to low pressure, they transfer kinetic energy through expansion, filling the available space until pressure levels stabilize. Therefore, for a vacuum to exist alongside high pressure, it requires a container or boundary to prevent this natural diffusion process.

This principle is fundamental in atmospheric science but does not apply to NASA. According to the top scientists of today, we have a high-pressure system, which is the air on planet Earth, right next to a perfect vacuum of space without any barrier or containment system. This is obviously impossible and goes against the current laws of thermodynamics. I believe that these satanic agendas are being pushed at any cost. The heliocentric model of the Earth is the result of the Big Bang, and evolution follows that. All of these teach that there is no God.

What is the Big Bang Theory?

This is what all students in state-run propaganda schools are taught. The Big Bang Theory is the leading scientific explanation for how the universe began. It proposes that the universe started about 13.8 billion years ago from an extremely hot, dense point (often referred to as a "singularity"). This point suddenly expanded or "exploded" in what we call the Big Bang, setting the universe into motion. This point was also reported to be the same size as a period on a page. According to this same pseudo-science, the universe is still rapidly expanding. The same scientists who believe in the Big Bang also believe in evolution. These are the same scientists who teach the Earth is a spinning globe in the vacuum of space. These so-called scientists are deniers of God and of his creation. This same scientist now also teaches that there are more than two genders.

The Big Bang theory was hatched by a Jesuit priest named Georges Lemaître. He joined the Society of Jesus (the Jesuits) in 1913 and was ordained in 1923. Lemaître's dual role as a scientist and a priest influenced his perspective on the relationship between science and faith, and he often sought to reconcile the two. His satanic religious background played a significant part in his philosophical views on the universe and its origins, particularly in how he approached the implications of his fake scientific findings.

Georges Lemaître was born on July 17, 1894, and he is often referred to as the father of the Big Bang theory. His theory laid the foundation for the modern understanding of the "universe's" origins.

In 1927, Lemaître proposed that the "universe" is expanding based on his supposed observations of distant galaxies. He suggested that if the "universe" is expanding, it must have originated from a single, extremely dense point, which he called the "primeval atom." This idea implied that the universe began with a "Big Bang," leading to the creation of matter and the cosmic expansion we observe today. Can you imagine that a priest would come up with such a ridiculous idea?

If you haven't figured it out by now, you can replace the word Jesuit with the word Satanic. So, all of our illustrious scientists of today believe this Big Bang theory that was imagined by a satanic Jesuit priest. This satanic Big Bang Theory is the stepping stone into another satanic lie called the theory of evolution.

What is the Theory of Evolution?

The theory of evolution as it pertains to human origins suggests that humans share a common ancestor with other primates, particularly the great apes. This theory claims that humans evolved through a long, gradual process over millions of years, shaped by natural selection and genetic adaptation. This, of course, is a satanic lie to lead people away from God.

Humans, along with chimpanzees, gorillas, and other primates, are believed to have a shared ancestor that lived approximately five to seven million years ago. Human evolution is supported by fake fossil records, fake DNA analysis, and false comparative studies with other primates, which show genetic and physical similarities pointing to a shared evolutionary history. All of this is satanic propaganda designed to teach people that there is no creator and that people are nothing more than a random accident.

The theory of evolution by natural selection was primarily developed by Charles Darwin, a British naturalist, who presented it in his groundbreaking work, On the Origin of Species, or The Preservation of Favoured Races in the Struggle for Life, published in 1859. Darwin's observations, gathered during his voyage on the ship HMS Beagle, led him to propose that species change over time through a process of natural selection, where organisms better adapted to their environment tend to survive and reproduce, passing on advantageous traits to their offspring. This, of course, is nothing but a satanic deception designed to keep people from learning the true story of creation. So old Charlie took a trip and saw many different animals, so his logical conclusion is that they all formed from nothing over millions of years. It sounds to me like he was demon-possessed because I don't believe that a man can come up with such a ridiculous, deluded notion on his own.

However, Charles Darwin acknowledged that the complexity of the human eye presented a challenge to his theory of evolution, as it seemed difficult to explain how such an intricate organ could evolve through natural selection. In *On the Origin of Species*, Darwin wrote:

"To suppose that the eye, with all its inimitable contrivances for adjusting the focus to different distances, for admitting different amounts of light, and for the correction of spherical and chromatic aberration, could have been formed by natural selection, seems, I freely confess, absurd in the highest possible degree."

Even Darwin himself admits that evolution is absurd to the highest possible degree. However, this satanic lie is still taught to children to this day and is believed by all the so-called scientists of today.

The Big Bang theory, evolution, and the concept of planets in outer space are linked in a way that suggests the universe, life, and humanity are products of random, natural processes without intentional design from God. According to this view, the Big Bang marks the origin of the universe from an initial explosion, leading to stars and planets, including Earth, forming by chance over billions of years. The theory of evolution then proposes that life began from simple organisms, evolving through random mutations and natural selection, ultimately producing humans as part of this process. This is the opposite of what the Bible teaches.

These satanic scientific explanations promote a worldview that denies a purposeful, divine creator, instead suggesting that life is a cosmic accident. This view can be seen as encouraging belief in a purposeless existence without inherent meaning. That is exactly what Satan wants. These are all false teachings designed to confuse you and keep you away from God. They are also designed to make you think you are nothing more than an accident with no significance at all.

If I told you that a frog could turn into a prince, you would know I was telling you a fairy tale. But that is what scientists believe today. They believe that a frog can turn into a prince, it just takes millions of years.

What are the Abyssal Plains?

The deep seafloor is one of the largest, least explored, and least understood habitats on Earth. The vast, flat, and muddy regions of the deep ocean floor, known as abyssal plains, cover more than 50% of Earth's surface. These plains are some of the flattest and smoothest areas on the entire planet.

From a Flat Earth perspective, the existence of such expansive, flat areas raises questions about the planet's true shape. How can such enormous, level plains exist on a spherical Earth, where curvature would theoretically disrupt these continuous flat surfaces? If the abyssal plains account for more than half of the Earth's surface, their vastness and flatness challenge the idea of a round planet, suggesting instead that the Earth's surface may indeed be flat—common sense.

Abyssal plains, with their consistent, smooth topography, align with the Flat Earth model. This raises the question: if more than half of the Earth's surface is incredibly flat, could this be further evidence that the Earth is flat, and have we been misled by the dominant spherical satanic model? The presence of these plains is just another undeniable proof of the true nature of Earth's surface.

Kenny Williamson

Earth Curvature Versus Perspective

The Earth's curvature calculations are based on the principles of geometry and trigonometry applied to a sphere. For a spherical Earth, one of the most commonly used formulas to calculate the curvature over a specific distance is based on the Pythagorean theorem:

According to scientists, the amount of Earth's curvature can be calculated as roughly 8 inches per mile squared (8 inches of drop for the first mile, 32 inches for two miles, 72 inches for three, and so on). This is something that should be easily observed.

Also, according to scientists, this supposed curvature becomes more apparent over vast distances, such as ocean horizons or large plains, which also aligns with observed phenomena like ships disappearing hull-first over the horizon. This, of course, sounds really good on paper, but any person can walk outside and look at a vast, large plain like the ocean and can clearly see with one's own eyes that it is flat, not curved.

This is propaganda at its finest. A person can look out over the ocean or the great salt plains and see that it looks as flat as a pancake. However, mainstream science says that you are looking at a curve. The mainstream scientists want you to ignore your God-given senses and believe whatever they tell you, regardless of what you can observe for yourself. They mention that one of the proofs that the Earth curves is that you can observe ships disappearing over the horizon hull first. This appears to be true at first glance because that is what your eyes tell you when looking for yourself. The human eye perceives distant objects based on a combination of its structure, the light reflecting off those objects, and the atmospheric conditions. The distance at which a person can see an object, especially at ground level, is generally limited to about three miles.

After Three miles, whatever you were looking at starts to disappear out of sight. Does that mean that the object you were looking at is gone? No, it is merely out of your sight. If you were to take something that magnifies your sight like a telescope, the object that you were looking at is still there. Again, it has just moved out of your sight. This is what perspective is as related to what you can see. In this case, the object you were looking at is gone from your perspective. It is still there, just too far for you to see. To me, this seems very easy to understand and common sense.

Now, you take this very simple observation of perspective and let a modern satanic scientist explain it to you. They will tell you that the object that you were watching has not just passed out of your line of sight, but it has now gone over the curve of the Earth, and it is on the other side of the curve. The reason that you cannot see this object anymore is because it is hidden behind the Earth itself. If, in this case, you were watching a ship sail away from you, at about three miles, the ship would appear to disappear slowly behind a wall of water caused by the Earth's curvature. If you consult any book, TV, or the internet, this is still what they teach and proclaim to this day.

However, not long ago, Nikon came out with a new camera with a lens that can zoom in up to 58 miles. It did not take long for people to start pointing these cameras at distant ships in the ocean sailing away and over the so-called curvature of the Earth. Amazingly enough, these ships that had disappeared over the curvature had now miraculously reappeared! Come to find out, these ships never disappeared at all; they merely sailed out far enough that the unaided human eye was unable to see them.

With this knowledge in hand, there are people all over the world taking these cameras and filming things that should be thousands of feet below the curvature of the Earth. They are seeing things that the scientists say you cannot see, but you can clearly see them. They are recording things that, according to the Earth's curvature calculator, should be impossible to see. This is happening because there is no curve; the Earth as we know it is a flat plane as far as any aided or unaided eye can see. This has been verified over and over with amateur rockets or balloons sent up as high as 120,000 feet above the surface of the Earth. When a regular lens camera is used, everything you see is flat. When NASA or some other satanic government does the same experiment, the Earth always has curvature. This is due to the lens being used on the camera. A regular lens shows how you see it with your eyes, and it is flat. They use a fish eye lens that distorts everything and shows a curvature. This is nothing more than trickery designed to fool you.

In October 2012, Felix Baumgartner jumped from a height of 127,852 feet (38,969 meters) during the Red Bull Stratos mission from a helium-filled balloon. You can see the video from this jump, and of course, it shows the Earth from that height with a pronounced curve. If you really pay attention, you can see that objects on the capsule being recorded are also distorted with a curve in the lettering. This is because they are using a fish eye lens. There is also a video of inside the capsule when the door opens. This camera is a regular camera without the fish eye lens. When the door opens, you can clearly see the Earth from that height is flat.

What Properties does a Vacuum have?

A vacuum is a space devoid of matter, meaning it has no particles such as air, gas, or other substances present. Because a vacuum lacks any medium (air, liquid, or solid), sound waves cannot travel through it. Sound requires a material to propagate, as it relies on the movement and vibration of particles. In air, for instance, sound waves move by compressing and expanding particles in a wave-like motion. Without particles in a vacuum to transfer this energy, sound has no medium to move through, making "space" silent.

This is very interesting because this vacuum proposes many problems for so-called space travel. When watching live stream videos from NASA astronauts working outside the space station, you can hear noise from the work being done. This, of course, should be impossible due to the fact that sound waves cannot travel in a vacuum.

Additionally, without particles, there is no air pressure or "wind" in a vacuum. Air pressure results from molecules of gas pushing against each other and any surrounding surfaces. Since a vacuum has no molecules to exert pressure, there is no movement of air in these regions.

This little fact also proposes many problems for space travel. What this means is as follows: There is no air or anything in a vacuum. There is no medium of any kind for anything to push against. Let me give you a very simple example that can be verified by anyone with a vacuum pump and a clear, airtight container that can support a vacuum. I saw this experiment done on a college campus. A battery-powered fan was placed in the container with a feather mounted to a rod opposite the fan. The fan was turned on, and you could clearly see the feather blowing in the wind. The vacuum pump was turned on, and it pulled the container into a vacuum. As the air was being evacuated from the container, the feather movement slowed and eventually stopped altogether. Even though the fan was still running aimed at the feather, the feather did not move because there was nothing the fan could push against, there was nothing to move the feather.

This very simple experiment shows some major flaws in NASA's little fake space game. The problem is that these rockets that you see blasting off to space are pushing against the air in order to have forward momentum. A rocket or jet engine only has thrust because it has air to push against. In a vacuum, there is no air; there is nothing for a rocket to push against. So, when you have a rocket in a vacuum, it behaves just like the aforementioned electric fan in a vacuum, it does nothing. There is not any medium at all for it to do anything with. So, how do these rockets from NASA manage to fly around in outer space? That is a very good question. I have the answer for you. They Don't.

It makes for a very entertaining show when you see a video of the space shuttle using its little thrusters in the vacuum of space to maneuver around. The only problem is you can't have thrust with nothing to push against. I can only assume that they are hoping that you never do any kind of research for yourself and that you simply believe every word that comes out of their satanic mouths.

When it comes to research, it is very hard to find the answers that you are looking for. All search engines have been scrubbed of anything that they don't want you to know. There are a few places and websites where you can go to learn the truth, but a Google search will only give you fake propaganda. Everything now is labeled disinformation, and our government wants anything other than their narrative to be wiped off the internet.

The First Journey to the

Edge of Space

In 1931, the brilliant Swiss physicist and explorer Auguste Piccard made history by becoming the first person to reach the Earth's stratosphere. With an interest in understanding the mysteries of our "planet," Piccard set out to explore the upper reaches of the atmosphere, where few believed humans could venture.

To achieve this feat, Piccard and his assistant built a specially designed pressurized capsule, which they suspended beneath a giant hydrogen balloon. This innovative setup allowed him to ascend nearly 10 miles above the Earth, reaching heights that were unprecedented at the time. This mission, intended for scientific research, would yield results that were both unexpected and controversial.

When Piccard returned, he shared his observations of the Earth as he saw it from this extraordinary height. To his surprise, and contrary to popular belief at the time, Piccard described the view of the Earth as a "flat disc with an upturned edge." His description, which appeared in Popular Science Magazine in August 1932, diverged significantly from the globe model that was widely accepted and taught. This is why you have probably never heard of him.

Piccard's statement on what he saw has led to ongoing debate, with some interpreting his observations as evidence challenging mainstream models of the Earth. However, what's undeniable is that his pioneering ascent provided the world with one of the earliest human perspectives from the edge of space. Today, Piccard's journey is omitted from all history books, but it is part of history nonetheless. This is just another example of anything that goes against the satanic narrative being squashed and never heard of again.

Kenny Williamson

Is the Moon Nothing More than Plasma?

In 1965, a little-known scientist named R. Foster captured the public's attention with a bold claim that challenged the very foundations of space science. Foster, who was introduced as a professor in a live interview, presented a radical theory: the Moon was not the rocky satellite scientists believed it to be, but rather a glowing sphere of plasma. If Foster was correct, his theory meant that a lunar landing would be not just difficult but outright impossible.

Foster explained that his findings, which he described as "profound and decisive," could necessitate a complete overhaul of conventional science and force a re-evaluation of the laws of physics. His claim was met with shock and disbelief. At a time when the "space race" was in full swing, and both the United States and the Soviet Union were competing to be the first to land on the Moon, Foster's plasma theory said that it couldn't be done.

The interview, aired live, caused a stir. It challenged the idea that humans would soon be able to explore the lunar surface. To Foster, the idea of landing on plasma, a form of matter that doesn't hold a solid shape, was inconceivable. His theory proposed that what people saw as the Moon was a sort of atmospheric phenomenon rather than a tangible object—just a lesser light placed in the firmament by God.

However, much of Foster's background is missing. A record in the ABC's production notebook from 1965 identifies him only as "FOSTER" and notes his Tasmanian origins. Beyond this, little documentation of his work or academic background can be found, making his identity and claims as elusive as his theory. Over time, Foster's plasma Moon hypothesis faded into obscurity, overshadowed by the fake 1969 Apollo Moon landing, when astronauts faked a landing on what appeared to be a solid lunar surface.

I am not surprised that Foster's work and background all disappeared. Foster was making the claim that the Moon was plasma right before NASA faked the Moon landing. Obviously, this could not be permitted; it may unravel the threads that were holding the fake Moon missions together. This man and his work were scrubbed from history.

I also believe that this lines up with the Bible when it describes the Moon as a light placed in the firmament. It is not a planet out in space. You cannot get to it or land on it.

Who Was Copernicus?

Nicolaus Copernicus (1473–1543) was a Polish mathematician, astronomer, and Jesuit best known for developing the heliocentric model of the universe. This revolutionary idea placed the Sun at the center of the universe rather than the Earth, challenging the long-accepted geocentric (Earth-centered) view. Remember, you can interchange the words Jesuit and Satanist.

Copernicus's theory said that Earth rotates daily on its axis and revolves around the Sun once a year, along with the other "planets." In 1543, shortly before his death, he published On the Revolutions of the Heavenly Spheres, laying the foundation for modern astronomy. This work sparked what would later be known as the Copernican Revolution and fueled the godless scientists to push the heliocentric model of the Earth.

His theory was at first thought to be inaccurate., but Copernicus always countered these inaccuracies by claiming his theories were merely scientific guesswork and shouldn't be considered truth.

In his book, he even wrote, "The Pythagorean teaching was founded upon hypothesis, and it is not necessary that the hypothesis should be true, or even probable. The hypothesis of the movement of the Earth is only one that is useful in explaining phenomena, but it should not be considered an absolute truth."

In other words, everything he wrote in his book could be completely false, and he admitted that. Even with his own statement that it was not to be taken as absolute truth, our scientists today teach it as absolute truth anyway. This is eerily like the confession of Charles Darwin that the evolution of the human eye is ridiculous, but they still teach it as absolute truth.

This is another example of God's truth compared to Satan's truth.

Kenny Williamson

Who Was Galileo?

Galileo and his predecessors, dedicated to promoting the heliocentric model, often developed complex theories to support their beliefs. A prime example of this was in 1616 when Galileo proposed his theory on the cause of tides. A year earlier, Cardinal Bellarmine had challenged Galileo, stating that the Copernican system could not be defended without solid, physical evidence that the Earth orbits the Sun rather than vice versa. Taking this to heart, Galileo attempted to show that Earth's tides were caused by the water's movement as the Earth supposedly accelerated and decelerated from its rotation and orbit around the Sun. He argued that this hypothetical "sloshing" of water was a direct result of Earth's motion, intending to use tides as proof of heliocentrism.

However, Galileo's idea was not well-received by his contemporaries, who pointed out that if his theory were correct, there would be only one high tide per day. Additionally, if Earth's motion caused the tides, all bodies of water—including lakes, ponds, and inland seas—should display similar tidal effects, which they do not. This inconsistency led many to question Galileo's theory as a definitive explanation for tides, but that didn't stop him.

Galileo, working to improve the telescope's magnification, managed to increase it from 3x to 30x, which allowed him to make what is considered his most significant discovery. Using his enhanced telescope, he claimed to have observed what he initially described as "three fixed stars" near Jupiter, which he could only see intermittently. By observing their changing positions, he concluded that these were not stars but Moons orbiting Jupiter, sometimes hidden behind the planet. Galileo argued that this observation supported the Copernican model, as it showed that other celestial bodies, like Jupiter, also had Moons orbiting them.

NASA continues to confirm these fake Moons' existence and claims to occasionally capture them with specialized telescopes. In other words, CGI. However, some question the existence of these Moons. With modern optics like the Nikon P900, boasting 83x optical and 332x digital zoom, these Moons have seemed to have disappeared. No one other than NASA and Galileo has ever seen these elusive Moons. This raises lots of questions about Galileo's initial observations. Galileo was rumored to be a Jesuit as well.

Who was Isaac Newton?

In 1687, Sir Isaac Newton published Principia Mathematica, introducing his concept of "gravity" to explain the unseen force that held objects to the Earth's surface. The globe-Earth model, at the time, faced scrutiny because the natural physics of spinning spheres would imply that anything on its surface should fall or fly off. How, then, could oceans, people, and structures remain securely attached to an Earth spinning faster than the speed of sound? That is still a good question.

To address these concerns, the globe-Earth model needed a force that was strong enough to keep the oceans and atmosphere held to Earth yet gentle enough to allow boats to float, birds to fly, and plants to grow unaffected. Newton proposed gravity as a universal magical force capable of acting over great distances, powerful enough to keep everything bound to the Earth but undetectable by any practical means of measurement of his time. His ideas met with criticism, as some viewed the notion of an "invisible force" as introducing mysticism into science, especially given its ability to act across empty space. Despite the criticism, Newton's theory of gravity became central to the scientific explanation of planetary and celestial motion.

According to the story behind Newton's theory of gravity, it all began when he observed an apple falling from a tree at Woolsthorpe Manor.

Unlike anyone before him, he was said to have had a breakthrough realization: the apple did not fall because it was heavier than air but because of an unseen force pulling it toward the Earth's center. Newton then developed his theory of universal gravitation, proposing that this force, "gravity," not only caused objects to fall but also governed the motions of celestial bodies.

Newton suggested that gravity was responsible for keeping Moons in orbit around planets and planets in orbit around stars, with the strongest gravitational pull coming from the most massive nearby bodies. Thus, at a human scale, gravity was supposedly what caused people, buildings, and oceans to stay grounded on Earth, while at a larger scale, it maintained the orbits of Moons and planets.

However, the theory raises questions: How could gravity act differently at different scales—keeping people fixed on Earth while simultaneously causing planets to orbit the Sun? This duality of gravity's effects remains a point of curiosity and debate, as it requires the same force to produce very different outcomes based on scale and context. For example, why has the Sun's gravity not pulled the Moon away from the Earth? They claim that the Sun is 100 times bigger than the Earth, yet the Earth's gravity is holding the Moon in place.

Who was Captain Cook?

In 1773, Captain James Cook became one of the earliest modern explorers to venture into the Antarctic Circle, embarking on a journey that inspired great intrigue around the mysteries of Antarctica and the potential shape of the Earth. His expedition aimed to fully circumnavigate Antarctica, with hopes of locating inlets or paths through the icy expanse. This voyage offered a unique opportunity to gather evidence supporting either the globe model or a Flat Earth model.

If the Earth were a globe with a 25,000-mile circumference at the equator, the coastline of Antarctica would measure approximately 12,000 miles. However, if Antarctica surrounded the Earth on a flat plane, the journey would extend over 50,000 miles along the ice wall that encircled the continents. Over three voyages spanning nearly three years, Captain Cook's crew sailed an astonishing 60,000 miles along the Antarctic coast, encountering only an unbroken wall of ice without finding any clear passage or end. In my opinion, proving a Flat Earth.

Captain Cook described the daunting ice barrier, writing, "The ice extended east and west far beyond the reach of our sight, while the southern half of the horizon was illuminated by rays of light reflected from the ice to a considerable height." Cook's observations left a profound impression on his crew and stirred debate about the true nature of Earth's geography.

Later explorations by Captain James Clark Ross and Captain George Nares in the 19th century strongly reinforced Captain Cook's observations regarding the southern glacial wall. Captain Ross, leading a multi-year expedition in heavily armored warships, searched the Antarctic coastline for over four years without finding an inlet or a way through the ice wall. Likewise, Captain Nares circumnavigated Antarctica for more than three years, logging nearly 69,000 miles along the way despite taking an indirect route.

For a relatively small ice continent, as suggested by globe Earth models, these expeditions would have completed their routes far sooner. However, the extensive mileage covered and the impenetrable ice boundary they encountered suggest a larger expanse, aligning with a Flat Earth model with Antarctica as a surrounding perimeter.

Additionally, explorers, including Captain Ross and Lieutenant Charles Wilkes, noted discrepancies in their positions when using globe Earth maps, often finding themselves 12-16 miles off course each day. These discrepancies increased to as much as 29 miles per day the farther south they traveled, which was puzzling, as strong currents and storms would logically impact their course in both directions, yet they consistently found themselves behind, not ahead, of schedule. This, of course, is consistent with the Flat Earth model. Time and time again, when these explorers have set out to prove a globe Earth, it always seems to cast even more doubt on the heliocentric model.

What about the Coriolis Effect?

In the mid-19th century, French scientist Gaspard-Gustave Coriolis conducted experiments on rotating systems, which resulted in what's now called the "Coriolis Effect." This concept has often been cited to support the heliocentric model, particularly with the claim that sinks and toilets in the Northern Hemisphere drain in one direction and in the opposite direction in the Southern Hemisphere, supposedly because of Earth's rotation. However, these household fixtures actually drain based on the shape of the basin and the direction of water flow, not Earth's spin.

Additionally, the Coriolis Effect is also used to explain bullet paths and weather patterns. For example, it is said to make long-range bullets curve right in the Northern Hemisphere and left in the Southern Hemisphere and cause storms to rotate in different directions depending on their location. However, such effects don't occur consistently enough to be definitive proof of Earth's rotation; not every bullet and storm follows this predicted behavior. In reality, these variations are influenced by local conditions rather than a universal force due to Earth's motion, again leaning towards a Flat Earth model and not a spinning globe.

Kenny Williamson

Are Satellites Real?

It's claimed there are over 20,000 satellites orbiting Earth in the thermosphere, where temperatures are said to exceed 4,530 degrees Fahrenheit. However, the metals used in satellites, such as aluminum, gold, and titanium, have melting points far below this threshold (1,221°F, 1,948°F, and 3,034°F, respectively), which raises questions about how they could withstand these extreme temperatures.

People often say they can see satellites with the naked eye, though this would be highly improbable, given that satellites are typically smaller than a bus and positioned over 100 miles away—too far for the eye to detect their shape or structure. Even through telescopes, satellites are not identified by shape but appear as passing lights, which could be mistaken for planes, drones, shooting stars, or other aerial objects.

Additionally, some satellites are "geostationary," meaning they supposedly remain fixed relative to a spot on Earth, which would imply they shouldn't move through the sky.

Did you know that most of the internet's infrastructure relies on ground-based cables, specifically fiber-optic cables? These cables form a complex network that connects data centers, internet service providers, and other key points across continents and under oceans. Although there are supposedly satellite internet systems, these are typically used in remote locations or for specialized purposes rather than serving as a primary backbone for the internet. Submarine cables, laid on the ocean floor, connect different continents and carry approximately 99% of international data traffic.

Fiber-optic cables are highly efficient for transmitting large amounts of data at high speeds over long distances, making them the preferred method for global internet connectivity. While satellites can supposedly help in rural or remote areas and for specific broadcasting applications, they generally cannot match the capacity, speed, and reliability of fiber-optic networks.

Many believe that instead of being positioned in outer space, satellites are mounted on high-altitude balloons. Proponents argue that helium balloons carrying technology for telecommunications, weather monitoring, and imaging provide the same functionality at lower costs, with fewer risks and more direct access than launching satellites via rockets.

Helium balloon-supported equipment is known to be used by agencies like NASA and various meteorological organizations for data collection and surveillance. These balloons can reach heights of up to 120,000 feet, placing them well above the typical cruising altitude of commercial flights and making them optimal for a fake space satellite hoax.

NASA is one of the world's largest consumers of helium. They are supposedly using all of this helium to purge rocket fuel and to cool equipment. I believe that they use this helium for high-altitude balloons. There is not a single picture that is not CGI of a satellite in outer space.

Kenny Williamson

What Properties Does Water Have?

Water and other liquids naturally settle into a flat and level state, demonstrating one of the core principles of fluid dynamics. When water is disturbed, it flows outward to find its new level as quickly as possible, aligning to a flat, even surface. This characteristic is visible everywhere—from still lakes to rushing rivers—which behave according to this principle regardless of location or scale.

Earth is a level plane, and water's tendency to find and remain level is expected and observable. Conversely, if Earth were a spinning globe, water would need to curve slightly to maintain a convex shape, a concept counterintuitive to fluid behavior. For instance, if the Earth is indeed a 25,000-mile-circumference sphere as widely proposed, large bodies of standing water should exhibit measurable curvature—a drop of 8 inches per mile squared.

Of course when tested, canals, lakes, and even larger water expanses appear level, with no detectable curvature, supporting the Flat Earth model.

Astronomers claim that gravity—a force stemming from the Earth's large mass—keeps everything, from oceans to people, adhered to the surface of the spinning globe. The idea is that Earth's mass creates a gravitational pull strong enough to hold the water, atmosphere, and everything else against it, even on the underside. However, this is not provable; it's all conjecture.

Take a wet tennis ball as an illustration: when you spin it, water flies off in all directions, showing an effect opposite to what's proposed for Earth's spinning sphere. Astronomers acknowledge this contrast, explaining that gravity only "kicks in" at a mass much larger than we can replicate, creating a situation where Earth supposedly keeps all water adhered tightly.

However, this goes against direct observation. Water naturally remains level and unaffected by the need for an invisible force to hold it in place, questioning the globe model's reliance on gravity to keep oceans stuck to the surface. As I have said before, gravity is strong enough to hold a ship upside down on the bottom of the Earth but weak enough to let birds fly off that same ship.

Are the Sun and the Moon the Same Size?

We're generally taught that the observed motions of the Sun, planets, and stars around Earth are optical illusions—except for the Moon. Modern explanations hold that the Earth is moving and that we only think these objects orbit around us due to this movement. However, the Moon is said to orbit Earth exactly as we see it, which is why it shows us only one side. This single-sided view is attributed to a "perfect match" between the Moon's slow west-to-east rotation of 10.3 mph and its orbital speed of 2,288 mph around Earth. These two speeds supposedly counter Earth's eastward rotation and orbit around the Sun, creating the "dark side" effect. They claim that the Moon is tidally locked to the Earth.

Though the Sun and Moon appear as similarly-sized bodies circling a stationary Earth, science tells us otherwise: we're taught that the Sun is 865,374 miles across, about 109 times Earth's width, while the Moon spans 2,159 miles. Both are seen as the same size from Earth only because the Moon is "relatively" nearby at 238,000 miles, compared to the Sun's immense distance of 93 million miles away. These numbers, we're told, just happen to create the impression that they're the same size from our perspective.

Again, this is propaganda designed for you to ignore what you can clearly see. The Sun and Moon look the same size because they are the same size. I believe that they are roughly the same size and are both following a circuit around the Earth. Both of these lights are very close to the Earth, very small compared to what the so-called scientists claim.

"Whilst we sit drinking our cup of tea or coffee, the world is supposedly rotating at 1,039 mph at the equator, whizzing around the Sun at 66,500 mph, hurtling towards Lyra at 20,000 mph, revolving around the center of the 'Milky Way' at 500,000 mph and merrily moving at God knows what velocity as a consequence of the 'Big Bang.' And not even a hint of a ripple on the surface of our tea, yet tap the table lightly with your finger and." -Neville T. Jones

What is the South Pole?

In the Flat Earth model, the South Pole is thought to be nonexistent, and Antarctica is instead described as a massive ice wall that circles the outer edge of Earth, containing the oceans within, like a giant "basin." Though this idea might seem unusual, proponents of this model assert that if one were to travel due south from any point on Earth, upon reaching approximately 78 degrees south latitude, they would encounter a vast ice wall rising 100 to 200 feet high and stretching endlessly east and west, forming the boundary of the known world.

In this perspective, Antarctica is not depicted as a small "ice continent" isolated at the bottom of the globe but rather as a massive ice barrier surrounding all continents, forming a natural boundary that holds the oceans in place. This concept raises intriguing questions that remain unresolved: How far does the Antarctic ice stretch outward? Is there an edge, or does it extend indefinitely? And what might lie beyond it?

Due to international treaties, military oversight, and restricted access, both the North Pole and Antarctica are largely off-limits to civilians, classified as "no-fly" and "no-sail" zones. There have even been accounts of civilian pilots and sea captains encountering strict restrictions, sometimes being turned back or escorted away under threat, emphasizing the layers of secrecy surrounding these regions.

"The ice-barrier, so frequently referred to in accounts of the Antarctic regions, is the forefront of the enormous glacier-covering, or ice-cap, which, accumulating in vast, undulating fields from the heavy snowfall, and ultimately attaining hundreds, if not thousands, of feet in thickness, creeps from the continent of Antarctica into the polar sea. The ice barrier, yet a part of the parent ice cap, presents itself to the navigator who has boldness enough to approach its fearful front as a solid, perpendicular wall of marble-like ice, ranging from one thousand to two thousand feet in thickness, of which from one hundred to two hundred feet rises above, and from eight hundred to eighteen hundred feet sinks below, the level of the sea." -Greely, General A. W. "Antarctica, or the Hypothetical Southern Continent." Cosmopolitan 17 (1894): p. 296

In this second section of the

book, we will take a look at

what the Bible has to say

about Flat Earth

Kenny Williamson

Walk in The Old Paths

Jer 6:16 Thus saith the LORD, Stand ye in the ways, and see, and ask for the old paths, where is the good way, and walk therein, and ye shall find rest for your souls. But they said, We will not walk therein.

The phrase "Stand ye in the ways, and see" encourages contemplation and reflection on the paths available to them. The "old paths" refer to the established moral and spiritual principles that have guided them in the past, which are associated with a "good way," leading to spiritual fulfillment, peace, and eternal salvation.

However, the people's response, "We will not walk therein," signifies their rejection of this call. It reflects a common theme in the Scriptures where the people turn away from divine guidance and truth, choosing instead to pursue their own paths or worldly desires, often leading to adverse consequences. This is exactly what we are seeing today. Most people have turned away from the Word of God and choose to believe atheist scientists.

This verse highlights the importance of seeking wisdom from the past and the consequences of ignoring such guidance. Most, if not all, ancients believed in the geocentric model of the Earth.

The Bible Predicts Fake Science

1Ti 6:20 O Timothy, keep that which is committed to thy trust, avoiding profane and vain babblings, and oppositions of science falsely so called:

In our current and future age of rapid scientific advancement and increasing knowledge, 1 Timothy 6:20 serves as a timeless reminder to maintain a discerning heart. Christians are called to engage with science and knowledge but with a critical awareness of ideas that, though labeled "science," may be "falsely so called"—ideas that deny spiritual realities or undermine the teachings of Scripture.

Faith and reason are not necessarily at odds; however, when "knowledge" leads to the rejection of God the Creator, the distortion of moral truth, or the undermining of the Gospel, it becomes a dangerous form of false science. Christians are called to hold fast to what is true, avoiding empty speculations and standing firm against ideas that oppose the knowledge of God.

I believe the heliocentric model of a "globe-shaped Earth" opposes the Biblical teaching of God. This is part of the satanic agenda.

Don't Learn the Ways of the Heathen

Jer 10:2 Thus saith the LORD, Learn not the way of the heathen, and be not dismayed at the signs of heaven; for the heathen are dismayed at them.

This verse can be interpreted by urging believers not to follow the "way of the heathen," suggesting that Christians should resist being swayed by the "signs of heaven" that are used to justify the modern scientific consensus on space, planets, and the nature of the Earth. For the Flat Earth believer, these scriptures affirm the importance of holding to the Bible's literal descriptions of creation. They encourage believers to resist what they see as the misleading teachings of modern science, viewing the Bible as the ultimate authority on the nature of the world.

This perspective challenges the prevailing scientific worldview and seeks to restore confidence in God's Word as the definitive source of truth, even when it contradicts mainstream heathen knowledge. Always remember that Satan is the god of this world, and he is a liar.

Bible Verses about the

Firmament

Let's get started with the verses of the Bible that pertain to Flat Earth. All of these verses are taken out of the Authorized Version, also known as the King James Bible.

Gen 1:1 In the beginning, God created the heaven and the Earth.

Starting with the very first verse in the Bible, we can only come to one obvious conclusion: God created the Earth before the Sun was created. Even though the verse says Heaven and Earth, that does not imply that the Sun was created first. It was not until Genesis 1:14 that the Sun was created. This, of course, contradicts the Big Bang theory.

Gen 1:2 And the Earth was without form, and void; and darkness was upon the face of the deep. And the Spirit of God moved upon the face of the waters.

Just as this verse implies, the Earth had no form as of yet. However, one can plainly see that there was a great deep. This deep is not the oceans of the Earth. This is the vast body of water that lies outside the Earth as we know it. This would be what the so-called scientists of our day refer to as "outer space." The Bible does not teach any vast vacuum of space. The Bible teaches that there is no space, so Satan teaches that there is an infinite space. Again, Satan is a liar.

Gen 1:6 And God said, Let there be a firmament in the midst of the waters, and let it divide the waters from the waters.

This verse is the first verse, which allows for the Flat Earth theory. As I have proven by Gen 1:2, the great void of vacuum that scientists claim exists is not empty space but water. Now, God has put a boundary in this water, calling it a firmament. This firmament is dividing the waters from the waters. God has installed an official boundary that separates our Earth from God's throne. We are not told what this firmament is made of, but it is described later in the Bible as hard as a molten looking glass.

Gen 1:7 And God made the firmament, and divided the waters which were under the firmament from the waters which were above the firmament: and it was so.

Our scientists claim that we are on a spinning ball in outer space, speeding at half a million miles an hour in an ever-expanding void. In this so-called space, there is no up or down. One can plainly see from this verse that up and down has been established even in the great waters of the deep. The firmament divides the waters above the firmament "up" from the waters under the firmament or "down." This is important to remember because, on the global Earth model or the heliocentric model, somebody is always upside down when comparing the northern hemisphere to the southern hemisphere. But for scientists to get around that obvious issue, they simply say there is no up or down in space.

Understanding the properties of water requires a physically hardened substance to keep it contained or separated. Thus, a dome/firmament is not only logical but is within the proper context of scripture.

Gen 1:8 And God called the firmament Heaven. And the evening and the morning were the second day.

In this verse, we can come to the conclusion that the firmament is not a thin, solid barrier. We can see that the firmament is thick enough to be called heaven, and we will see that in this firmament is where God placed the Sun and the Moon and all of the luminaries that the scientists referred to as stars. I believe that it is this firmament that separates us from the deep. In this firmament are where the stars are that we see at night. When we are told we are looking into outer space, we are actually looking into the firmament. Beyond the firmament is the deep where God has placed his throne. We don't know if the Sun and Moon are spherical or flat and round. Scientists claim they are spherical planets in outer space. No one has ever seen the other side of the Moon or the Sun.

Gen 1:9 And God said, Let the waters under the heaven be gathered together unto one place, and let the dry land appear: and it was so.

In this verse, we can deduce that if the Earth is indeed a flat plane, it is not an indefinite one. We read that the waters under the firmament were gathered together in one place. This is where we imagine the dome over the Flat Earth. It stands to reason that if the deep is infinite, the firmament must have an end to be able to encompass the water and dry land that has been gathered together. This dome firmament is not only encompassing the gathered together Earth, but it's also separating the Earth from the deep.

Gen 1:10 And God called the dry land Earth; and the gathering together of the waters called he Seas: and God saw that it was good.

This verse simply explains what we have already discovered. The dry land that has been gathered together under the firmament is called Earth. This is the name given to the dry land, not to a planet floating in outer space. There is no "planet" Earth. Earth is the name for the dry land under the firmament. The water that has been gathered is called the Sea. This is not the deep; the deep is outside the firmament. Some of our seas are very deep, but nothing compared to the Great Deep.

Gen 1:14 And God said, Let there be lights in the firmament of the heaven to divide the day from the night; and let them be for signs, and for seasons, and for days, and years:

Here, we have the commandment for the lights to be placed in the firmament. They are not above it nor below it. They are in it. These lights, based on their description, are the Sun, the Moon, the stars, and the wandering stars. There are no planets floating in a vacuum of space, as science fiction movies portray. There are lights in the sky that scientists claim to be planets in outer space, but of course, this is not a biblical teaching. The Bible teaches that the lights we see are for seasons and for days and years. They are all in the firmament, not in outer space. These luminaries are moving in their circuit around the Earth, not vice versa.

Gen 1:15 And let them be for lights in the firmament of the heaven to give light upon the Earth: and it was so.

These luminaries, like the Sun and Moon, were placed in the firmament for the sole purpose of giving light to the Earth. The Bible does not discuss what these luminaries are made of. But I believe that the planets as NASA describes them are totally false in every respect.

Gen 1:16 And God made two great lights; the greater light to rule the day, and the lesser light to rule the night: he made the stars also.

Here, we see that out of all the lights that were placed in the firmament, there are two that are two great lights. The greater light is obviously the Sun, and the lesser light is obviously the Moon. Just as described, these are two individual lights. They are both light sources. The Moon is not reflecting Sunlight; the Moon is its own light. The light reflecting off of the Moon is based on the heliocentric model, where the Earth is a globe revolving around the Sun. This is not Biblical teaching. The Bible clearly teaches that the Sun is nothing more than a light placed in the firmament. The same goes for the Moon, of course. I believe the Sun and the Moon are very close to the same size.

Gen 1:17 And God set them in the firmament of the heaven to give light upon the Earth,

Gen 1:18 And to rule over the day and over the night, and to divide the light from the darkness: and God saw that it was good.

These two verses again describe the purpose of the two great lights. The greater of the two lights rules over the day, and the lesser of the two rules over the night. It also reiterates that these two lights were placed in the firmament. Knowing that Earth is a gathering of land under the firmament, and the Sun and Moon are in the firmament. There is no way to conclude that the Earth is a planetoid in a vacuum of space rotating around the Sun. In fact, one should conclude that the Sun is rotating in and around the firmament above the Earth. This is the opposite of what "science" so-called indoctrinates the masses with today.

Gen 1:20 And God said, Let the waters bring forth abundantly the moving creature that hath life, and fowl that may fly above the Earth in the open firmament of heaven.

In this verse, we notice that the birds may fly above the Earth in the open firmament of heaven. We know that God called the firmament heaven. We know that God placed the Sun, Moon, and stars in the firmament as well. We also know that birds can't fly that high. I have concluded that the area under the main portion of the firmament between the stars and the Earth is the air that we breathe, which is referred to here as the open firmament. I don't believe that the luminaries are in the open portion of the firmament but in a portion that man cannot penetrate. Because this verse specifies the open firmament of heaven is where the birds fly, I think the logical conclusion is that the firmament where the luminaries reside is a closed firmament. We cannot get in it or through it.

Gen 7:11 In the six hundredth year of Noah's life, in the second month, the seventeenth day of the month, the same day were all the fountains of the great deep broken up, and the windows of heaven were opened.

This is a reference to the great flood of Noah. In the Flat Earth model, you have water above the firmament, and you have water below the Earth called the Great Deep. I believe that this water flows in and out of the great deep and supplies our oceans with fresh water all the time. It is this in-and-out flow that causes the tides in the ocean and not the Moon. God is able to open a window or door in the firmament at his will. In this passage, God did just that and allowed water to rush in and flood the entire Earth. He also allowed more water to flow from the great deep under the Earth. This far surpassed the normal amount that controls the tides. The result was that the Earth was flooded, and all of mankind was drowned, save Noah and his family.

Gen 8:2 The fountains also of the deep and the windows of heaven were stopped, and the rain from heaven was restrained;

This is just the proof text that when God was finished flooding the Earth, he then closed the windows in the firmament, and the water no longer rushed in. God and his angels can pass through the firmament to get from heaven to Earth, but man cannot.

Job 9:8 Which alone spreadeth out the heavens, and treadeth upon the waves of the sea

From a Flat Earth viewpoint, this phrase can be understood as describing the firmament—an ancient concept of the sky as a solid structure that God spread out over the Earth. Proponents of the Flat Earth model often interpret biblical references to the heavens being "spread out" as a flat, horizontal plane rather than the curved expanse associated with a globe. This reinforces the idea that the heavens (or firmament) stretch out over a Flat Earth, which aligns with ancient Hebrew cosmology, where the Earth was perceived as flat and covered by the firmament.

Job 26:7 He stretcheth out the north over the empty place, and hangeth the Earth upon nothing.

I believe that the Earth is firmly established by God, needing no physical support because it is sustained by His will and power alone. The Earth doesn't float in space but is set upon an immovable foundation, as described in other biblical passages.

For those who hold a Flat Earth perspective, this verse can be seen as affirming God's deliberate creation of a flat, stationary Earth, which He sustains by His power. The imagery of God stretching out the north over an empty place and hanging the Earth "upon nothing" points to a divinely established world, secure in His hands, without the need for it to be spinning or moving through space.

Job 37:18 Hast thou with him spread out the sky, which is strong, and as a molten looking glass?

This verse comes from a speech by Elihu in the Book of Job, where he is praising God's power and wisdom in creation. Elihu emphasizes the majesty of God's work, particularly in the formation of the sky. When interpreted from a Flat Earth perspective, this verse provides strong imagery that resonates with the idea of a Flat Earth and a solid, dome-like firmament covering it.

The phrase "spread out the sky" aligns closely with the Flat Earth belief that the sky, or firmament, is a solid, dome-like structure that God spread over the Flat Earth. According to ancient Hebrew cosmology, the sky was not seen as an infinite expanse of space but rather a firm, tangible barrier separating the waters above from the Earth below (as mentioned in Genesis 1:6-8). From a Flat Earth perspective, this description fits with the idea of a fixed, protective dome that covers the Earth.

In this interpretation, the act of "spreading out" the sky reflects God's deliberate and careful construction of the heavens, laying them over the Earth like a canopy, perfectly designed to protect and enclose the world. It highlights God's authority as the Creator, who shaped the Earth in a specific and ordered way.

The reference to the sky being "strong" supports the idea of a firmament, a solid structure with real substance, rather than an atmospheric or abstract concept. In Flat Earth interpretations, this phrase reinforces the belief that the firmament is a physical barrier capable of withstanding immense forces. It is not fragile or thin, but rather "strong"—a robust, unshakable dome that protects the Earth and its inhabitants.

This strength of the sky, or firmament, speaks to the durability and immovability of the Flat Earth model, where everything is held together by divine design. The firmament's strength symbolizes God's unbreakable covenant with creation, ensuring that the Earth remains stable and secure under His care.

The phrase "as a molten looking glass" describes the sky as something smooth, reflective, and brilliantly crafted much like polished metal or glass. In the Flat Earth model, this is often interpreted as the firmament being a solid, reflective dome. The comparison to a "molten looking glass" suggests a surface that is both beautiful and impenetrable. The stars, Sun, and Moon are embedded within this dome, reflecting light across the Earth.

For Flat Earth proponents, this verse serves as a vivid description of the firmament's appearance—shiny, polished, and firm, much like ancient views of the heavens as a solid, shimmering barrier. It highlights not only the physical structure of the firmament but also the beauty and craftsmanship with which God created it.

Job 37:18 reinforces the idea that the Earth is covered by a firm, solid sky—a firmament—carefully and intentionally spread out by God. The imagery of the sky being strong and like a molten looking glass supports the notion of a solid dome that is both protective and reflective. This is exactly what you would expect in the Flat Earth model, where the Earth is stationary, covered by a firmament that God placed to separate the waters above from the Earth below.

The sky is not an infinite, empty expanse leading to outer space, but a strong and carefully crafted barrier, reflecting the glory of God's handiwork. Job 37:18 serves as a beautiful affirmation of a Flat Earth enclosed by a firmament.

Psa 19:1 To the chief Musician, A Psalm of David. The heavens declare the glory of God; and the firmament sheweth his handywork.

The "heavens" (the sky and celestial bodies) demonstrate God's majesty. The observable sky, stars, Sun, and Moon are seen as perfect examples of God's design and purpose. The regularity and precision of celestial movements, in this interpretation, display God's intentional handiwork. Not accidents caused by the Big Bang.

The firmament, believed in this model to be a literal, tangible dome, could be viewed as a protective covering carefully constructed by God. It shows God's intimate involvement in creating a world where everything fits harmoniously. The fact that it "sheweth his handiwork" would highlight God's craftsmanship, emphasizing that every detail of the Earth's structure—including the firmament—is a reflection of His design. This, of course, would confirm that the Earth was created with intelligent design.

Psa 148:4 Praise him, ye heavens of heavens, and ye waters that be above the heavens.

For those who believe the firmament was destroyed after the flood, it is important to consider Psalm 148:4, where King David proclaims, "Praise him, ye heavens of heavens, and ye waters that be above the heavens." This shows that the firmament and the waters above it still exist after the flood, affirming that the firmament was not destroyed. There were approximately three hundred years between the flood of Noah and When David became King. In Genesis 1:6-8, God created the firmament to separate the waters above from those below, and these same waters remained intact even after Noah's flood.

This evidence indicates that the firmament continues to hold back the waters above the Earth, functioning as it did from the moment of creation. David's psalms serve as a reminder of the firmament's enduring presence and role in reflecting the grandeur of God's creation, signifying that the heavens and firmament still declare His glory unchanged and undiminished, even after the flood. Do you really believe the atheist scientists of today who claim there is no firmament?

Psa 150:1 Praise ye the LORD. Praise God in his sanctuary: praise him in the firmament of his power.

In this verse, the firmament is seen as a mighty work of God, something that displays His omnipotence and sovereignty. The firmament is not just a physical barrier but a demonstration of God's power, holding back the waters above and maintaining the structure of creation.

Pro 8:28 When he established the clouds above: when he strengthened the fountains of the deep:

The "fountains of the deep" refer to the waters that flow from beneath the Earth, often associated with underground springs, rivers, and seas. In the Flat Earth interpretation, this idea of waters beneath the Earth holds significance, aligning with beliefs that the Earth is supported by vast reservoirs of water below, similar to the descriptions in Genesis of the flood and the deep waters.

God established and strengthened these waters, meaning He provided a reliable source of life-sustaining water for the Earth. From a Flat Earth perspective, these "fountains of the deep" reflect a well-ordered system where water flows beneath the Earth, contributing to the balance of creation. These waters also control the tides in the oceans, constantly replenishing them.

Pro 8:29 When he gave to the sea his decree, that the waters should not pass his commandment: when he appointed the foundations of the Earth:

Part of this verse refers to God's command to set boundaries for the seas, ensuring that the waters do not cross the limits He established. From a Flat Earth viewpoint, this could align with the concept of the ice wall, often believed to be a barrier of ice surrounding the edges of the Flat Earth. In this model, the ice wall is considered the boundary that keeps the oceans contained, preventing the waters from overflowing the edges of the Earth.

The ice wall (which some equate with Antarctica or an impenetrable ice boundary) could be seen as a physical manifestation of God's commandment to the sea. It functions as the divinely established barrier, ensuring that the oceans remain within the limits God intended just as God "decrees" the boundaries for the sea, this ice wall could be viewed as the structure that enforces His commandment in a practical sense.

The idea that the waters "should not pass his commandment" speaks to God's ultimate power and control over the elements of creation. From this perspective, the sea's obedience to God's decree, enforced by the ice wall, underscores His sovereignty over the natural world. It emphasizes that no force of nature can act outside the boundaries God has set, which, from a Flat Earth view, includes the waters being contained within the circular perimeter of the Earth.

Isa 40:22 It is he that sitteth upon the circle of the Earth, and the inhabitants thereof are as grasshoppers; that stretcheth out the heavens as a curtain, and spreadeth them out as a tent to dwell in:

The phrase "circle of the Earth" is often debated between Flat Earth and spherical Earth interpretations. In a Flat Earth view, this "circle" refers not to a globe but rather to a circular, flat plane, as Flat Earth proponents believe the Earth is shaped. The circle could be understood as the circular perimeter or boundary of the Flat Earth, sometimes depicted as being surrounded by the ice wall (often equated with Antarctica).

From this perspective, God is depicted as sitting above this circular plane, which emphasizes His supremacy over the Earth. The fact that He "sits upon" the Earth suggests that He is overseeing all creation from a position of authority. It reinforces the belief that the Earth, being a specially designed, circular plane, is directly under God's watchful care.

From the Flat Earth perspective, God looks down from above the firmament and sees the entire Earth—its circular form and its inhabitants. The comparison of humans to grasshoppers symbolizes how vast the Earth appears from God's perspective and reinforces His supremacy over both the Earth and its inhabitants. Man is very small and insignificant compared to God.

The tent imagery used here could be seen as reinforcing the idea that the Earth and its inhabitants are enclosed within a protective dome or structure. The firmament is often described as a kind of tent-like covering stretched out over the Earth, creating a contained, livable environment.

Isa 42:5 Thus saith God the LORD, he that created the heavens, and stretched them out; he that spread forth the Earth, and that which cometh out of it; he that giveth breath unto the people upon it, and spirit to them that walk therein:

Isaiah 42:5 can be interpreted as a celebration of God's purposeful and thoughtful creation. In a Flat Earth context, this verse emphasizes God's role in stretching out the heavens (the firmament) and spreading forth the Earth as a flat, stable plane where all life is sustained by His power. The Earth is viewed as a perfectly crafted environment where God gives life and breath to humanity, affirming His care and sovereignty over all creation.

Isa 44:24 Thus saith the LORD, thy redeemer, and he that formed thee from the womb, I am the LORD that maketh all things; that stretcheth forth the heavens alone; that spreadeth abroad the Earth by myself;

This verse highlights God as the Creator and Redeemer who formed humanity and made all things. This verse emphasizes God's sovereignty in stretching forth the heavens and spreading abroad the

Earth as a flat, expansive plane. This portrayal reinforces the belief that God intentionally crafted the Earth as a stable and livable environment. His solitary act of creation signifies His power and wisdom, establishing a well-ordered world where humanity thrives, reflecting His care and purpose in all aspects of life. This is completely opposite of the satanic Big Bang theory.

Isa 45:12 I have made the Earth, and created man upon it: I, even my hands, have stretched out the heavens, and all their host have I commanded.

This verse declares God as the Creator of the Earth and humanity, emphasizing He is the creator. This verse highlights that God made the Earth as a stable, flat plane designed for human life. His act of stretching out the heavens signifies the firmament that protects and encompasses the Earth, showcasing His sovereignty over all creation. The phrase "all their host have I commanded" reflects His authority over the universe, ensuring that everything functions according to His divine plan, affirming His care for humanity within this thoughtfully crafted world. Again, this is the opposite of the satanic Big Bang theory.

Isa 48:13 Mine hand also hath laid the foundation of the Earth, and my right hand hath spanned the heavens: when I call unto them, they stand up together.

Isaiah 48:13 emphasizes God's power in laying the foundations of the Earth and spanning the heavens. This verse highlights that God meticulously designed the Earth with a solid, stable foundation, creating a flat plane that supports life. The imagery of His hand spanning the heavens suggests a protective firmament above, reinforcing the idea that the heavens are thoughtfully arranged around the Earth. When God calls, the heavens respond, illustrating His authority and the harmonious order of creation, where everything functions according to His divine purpose and design. The Earth is the center of all of God's creation.

Ezk 1:22 And the likeness of the firmament upon the heads of the living creature was as the colour of the terrible crystal, stretched forth over their heads above.

Ezekiel 1:22 describes the firmament as a magnificent and crystal-like expanse stretched over the heads of these living creatures. This verse highlights the idea of the firmament as a beautiful, protective dome that encompasses the Flat Earth. The imagery of the firmament being "stretched forth" suggests a deliberate design by God, creating a stable and secure environment for all living beings. This portrayal reinforces the belief in a well-ordered creation, where the heavens not only protect but also reflect God's glory and majesty above the Earth.

Ezk 1:23 And under the firmament were their wings straight, the one toward the other: every one had two, which covered on this side, and every one had two, which covered on that side, their bodies.

Ezk 1:24 And when they went, I heard the noise of their wings, like the noise of great waters, as the voice of the Almighty, the voice of speech, as the noise of an host: when they stood, they let down their wings.

Ezk 1:25 And there was a voice from the firmament that was over their heads, when they stood, and had let down their wings.

Ezk 1:26 And above the firmament that was over their heads was the likeness of a throne, as the appearance of a sapphire stone: and upon the likeness of the throne was the likeness as the appearance of a man above upon it.

The verses from Ezekiel 1:23-26 vividly describe a vision of God's glory, focusing on His throne positioned above the firmament:

Ezekiel 1:23 depicts the wings of living creatures under the firmament, symbolizing their service and readiness to carry out God's will. Their wings are spread out, showcasing the dynamic nature of creation beneath God's authority.

Ezekiel 1:24 describes the powerful sound of their wings, likening it to the noise of great waters and the voice of the Almighty.

Ezekiel 1:25 highlights that there was a voice from the firmament above their heads, indicating communication from God, further reinforcing that His throne is above the firmament.

Ezekiel 1:26 culminates in the revelation of God's throne above the firmament, described as resembling a sapphire stone. This imagery underscores God's supreme sovereignty, with His throne as the central point of His divine rule and glory.

Together, these verses emphasize that God's throne is exalted above the firmament, symbolizing His ultimate authority and the structured order of creation. The firmament serves as a boundary, with God reigning from His heavenly throne, commanding all that lies beneath, reflecting His power and majesty in the universe.

Not exactly what you would find in the heliocentric model.

Ezk 10:1 Then I looked, and, behold, in the firmament that was above the head of the cherubims there appeared over them as it were a sapphire stone, as the appearance of the likeness of a throne.

Ezekiel 10:1 describes a vision where, above the cherubim, a stunning sapphire-like throne appears in the firmament. From a Flat Earth perspective, this verse highlights the idea of the firmament as a majestic, protective dome over the Earth, emphasizing God's divine presence and authority. The imagery of the throne, resembling a precious stone, signifies God's sovereignty and His exalted position above creation. This portrayal fosters a sense of awe and reverence, suggesting that God's throne is a source of power and order, overseeing the Earth and all life within it, reinforcing the belief in a well-structured universe under His care.

Dan 12:3 And they that be wise shall shine as the brightness of the firmament; and they that turn many to righteousness as the stars for ever and ever.

Daniel 12:3 states that those who are wise will shine like the brightness of the firmament, and those who lead others to righteousness will shine like the stars forever. This verse can be interpreted positively by emphasizing the firmament as a magnificent, radiant canopy above the Earth, symbolizing divine glory and truth.

Amo 9:6 It is he that buildeth his stories in the heaven, and hath founded his troop in the Earth; he that calleth for the waters of the sea, and poureth them out upon the face of the Earth: The LORD is his name.

Amos 9:6 emphasizes God's sovereignty as the Creator, stating that He builds His stories in the heavens and has founded His troop on the Earth. This verse underscores the idea that the Earth has a flat face, where God's foundational work is established.

The phrase "poureth them out upon the face of the Earth" highlights the concept of a flat surface, suggesting that God has designed the Earth as a stable and level plane. This imagery reinforces the belief that the Earth is intentionally crafted, where the heavens and Earth interact in a harmonious relationship. The mention of God's authority in calling for the waters of the sea further affirms His control over creation, demonstrating that everything functions according to His divine will. Ultimately, this verse celebrates the structured nature of the universe, where God's name signifies His unmatched power over all things.

Act 7:56 And said, Behold, I see the heavens opened, and the Son of man standing on the right hand of God

Acts 7:56 recounts the moment when Stephen proclaims, "Behold, I see the heavens opened, and the Son of Man standing on the right hand of God." Emphasizing that the opening of the heavens refers to the firmament, this verse suggests a divine revelation where the protective dome above is momentarily lifted to reveal the glory of God.

In this context, the firmament serves as a barrier between the Earthly realm and the heavenly, indicating that God's presence is both above and intimately involved in creation. Stephen's vision symbolizes a profound connection between Earth and the divine, illustrating that beyond the firmament lies the exalted position of Jesus, affirming His authority and majesty. This imagery inspires awe and hope, suggesting that through faith, believers can glimpse the spiritual realities beyond the physical world, underscoring the significance of the firmament as a gateway to divine truth and communion with God.

Rev 4:6 And before the throne there was a sea of glass like unto crystal: and in the midst of the throne, and round about the throne, were four beasts full of eyes before and behind.

In Revelation 4:6, the "sea of glass like unto crystal" is described as being before the throne of God, symbolizing something vast, clear, and still. This imagery can be interpreted as representing a calm, transparent sea of water above the firmament, separating the heavens from the Earth. The stillness of this sea, like glass or crystal, suggests a boundary or firm layer, reinforcing the idea of a fixed, unchanging firmament that holds the waters above. Again, this verse mentions a sea of glass before God's throne. God's throne sets on this sea of glass, not in the vastness of outer space.

Rev 6:13 And the stars of heaven fell unto the Earth, even as a fig tree casteth her untimely figs, when she is shaken of a mighty wind.

Revelation 6:13 states, "And the stars of heaven fell unto the Earth, even as a fig tree casteth her untimely figs, when she is shaken of a mighty wind." This verse can be interpreted to emphasize that the stars, often thought of as distant planets in space, are depicted here as being closely related to the Earth.

The imagery of stars falling to the Earth like figs shaken from a tree suggests that they are not celestial bodies in a vast, empty universe but rather entities that interact with the Earth in a more immediate way. This perspective supports the idea that stars are part of the firmament above, emphasizing their presence as components of a structured and orderly creation. In several places in the Bible, Angels are referred to as stars. In this verse, it could also mean that certain Angels fall down from heaven to Earth. When we see stars, are we actually seeing Angels?

Rev 6:14 And the heaven departed as a scroll when it is rolled together; and every mountain and island were moved out of their places.

Revelation 6:14 describes a dramatic event where "the heaven departed as a scroll when it is rolled together," and mountains and islands were moved. This verse emphasizes the firmament, which is seen as the heavens above the Earth, rolling back like a scroll. This imagery reinforces the idea of the firmament being a physical, structured dome that can be opened or altered. This could not happen on the heliocentric model of the Earth.

The moving of mountains and islands suggests that the Earth's surface, viewed as a flat plane, undergoes a profound shift under God's command. This scene underscores God's absolute power and control over both the heavens and the Earth, symbolizing a moment of divine intervention. It reflects a positive view of a Flat Earth by portraying a well-ordered creation in which the firmament and the Earth are intricately connected, all subject to God's will, revealing His ultimate authority and the importance of His design.

If there is no firmament, it makes God out to be a liar. God's word plainly teaches there is a firmament. NASA claims there is no firmament. Who do you think is the liar?

The Universe is Complete

Gen 2:1 Thus the heavens and the Earth were finished, and all the host of them.

Genesis 2:1 declares, "Thus the heavens and the Earth were finished, and all the host of them." This verse emphasizes that God's act of creation was complete and final. From this perspective, creation is not an ongoing, expanding process but a finished, perfectly designed work. The heavens and the Earth, along with everything within them, were created in a fully formed and functional state, showcasing God's perfection and purpose.

This reinforces the belief that the universe, including the Earth and the firmament, is stable and not subject to continuous change or expansion, as modern scientific theories like the expanding universe suggest. Instead, creation was completed in its entirety, reflecting the finality of God's work and His sovereign control over a well-ordered, finished world. There was no Big Bang.

The Earth has a Face or a Flat Geometrical Surface

The Bible contains multiple verses that refer to the"face of the Earth,"
a term that implies a geometrical flat surface. In passages like Genesis
1:29, Genesis 6:7, Genesis 11:4, and many others, the Earth is
consistently described with the word "face," which in geometry refers
to a flat, level surface. While the Earth features mountains, valleys,
and canyons, these are seen as variations on an otherwise level plane,
not evidence of a spherical shape.

In Genesis 1:29, God declares, "Behold, I have given you every herb
bearing seed, which is upon the face of all the Earth," indicating a flat
plane on which resources are distributed. Similarly, in Genesis 6:7,
God says He will "destroy man whom I have created from the face of
the Earth," implying that humanity inhabits a single, continuous, flat
surface. In Genesis 11:4, the builders of the Tower of Babel speak of
building a tower whose top may reach unto heaven, located on the face
of the Earth, which reinforces the idea of a broad, flat surface as a
foundation.

Other verses, such as Exodus 32:12 and Job 37:12, also use the phrase
"face of the Earth" to describe the entire inhabited world. These
scriptures collectively describe the Earth as having a geometrical flat
face, not a rotating sphere. The use of "face" supports the view of the
Earth as a flat expanse, with mountains and canyons being local

features but the overall design being flat and level. This interpretation aligns with the Flat Earth model, suggesting that the Bible describes the Earth as a stable, unchanging surface, spread out for life to flourish upon it, rather than as a globe formed by an accidental explosion.

These verses are listed in detail :

*Gen 1:29 And God said, Behold, I have given you every herb bearing seed, which is upon the **face of all the Earth**, and every tree, in the which is the fruit of a tree yielding seed; to you it shall be for meat.*

*Gen 4:14 Behold, thou hast driven me out this day from the **face of the Earth**; and from thy face shall I be hid; and I shall be a fugitive and a vagabond in the Earth; and it shall come to pass, that every one that findeth me shall slay me.*

*Gen 6:1 And it came to pass, when men began to multiply on the **face of the Earth**, and daughters were born unto them,*

*Gen 6:7 And the LORD said, I will destroy man whom I have created from the **face of the Earth**; both man, and beast, and the creeping thing, and the fowls of the air; for it repenteth me that I have made them.*

*Gen 7:3 Of fowls also of the air by sevens, the male and the female; to keep seed alive upon the **face of all the Earth**.*

*Gen 7:4 For yet seven days, and I will cause it to rain upon the Earth forty days and forty nights; and every living substance that I have made will I destroy from off the **face of the Earth**.*

*Gen 8:9 But the dove found no rest for the sole of her foot, and she returned unto him into the ark, for the waters were on the **face of the whole Earth**: then he put forth his hand, and took her, and pulled her in unto him into the ark.*

*Gen 11:8 So the LORD scattered them abroad from thence upon the **face of all the Earth**: and they left off to build the city.*

*Gen 11:9 Therefore is the name of it called Babel; because the LORD did there confound the language of all the Earth: and from thence did the LORD scatter them abroad upon the **face of all the Earth**.*

*Gen 41:56 And the famine was over all the **face of the Earth**: And Joseph opened all the storehouses, and sold unto the Egyptians; and the famine waxed sore in the land of Egypt.*

*Exo 32:12 Wherefore should the Egyptians speak, and say, For mischief did he bring them out, to slay them in the mountains, and to consume them from the **face of the Earth**? Turn from thy fierce wrath, and repent of this evil against thy people.*

*Exo 33:16 For wherein shall it be known here that I and thy people have found grace in thy sight? is it not in that thou goest with us? so shall we be separated, I and thy people, from all the people that are upon the **face of the Earth**.*

*Num 12:3 (Now the man Moses was very meek, above all the men which were upon the **face of the Earth**.)*

*Deu 6:15 (For the LORD thy God is a jealous God among you) lest the anger of the LORD thy God be kindled against thee, and destroy thee from off the **face of the Earth**.*

*Deu 7:6 For thou art an holy people unto the LORD thy God: the LORD thy God hath chosen thee to be a special people unto himself, above all people that are upon **the face of the Earth**.*

*1Sa 20:15 But also thou shalt not cut off thy kindness from my house for ever: no, not when the LORD hath cut off the enemies of David every one from **the face of the Earth**.*

*1Ki 13:34 And this thing became sin unto the house of Jeroboam, even to cut it off, and to destroy it from off the **face of the Earth**.*

*Job 37:12 And it is turned round about by his counsels: that they may do whatsoever he commandeth them upon the **face of the world** in the Earth.*

*Psa 104:30 Thou sendest forth thy spirit, they are created: and thou renewest the **face of the Earth**.*

*Jer 25:26 And all the kings of the north, far and near, one with another, and all the kingdoms of the world, which are upon the **face of the Earth**: and the king of Sheshach shall drink after them.*

*Jer 28:16 Therefore thus saith the LORD; Behold, I will cast thee from off the **face of the Earth**: this year thou shalt die, because thou hast taught rebellion against the LORD.*

*Ezk 34:6 My sheep wandered through all the mountains, and upon every high hill: yea, my flock was scattered upon all the **face of the Earth**, and none did search or seek after them.*

*Ezk 38:20 So that the fishes of the sea, and the fowls of the heaven, and the beasts of the field, and all creeping things that creep upon the Earth, and all the men that are upon the **face of the Earth**, shall shake at my presence, and the mountains shall be thrown down, and the steep places shall fall, and every wall shall fall to the ground.*

*Ezk 39:14 And they shall sever out men of continual employment, passing through the land to bury with the passengers those that remain upon the **face of the Earth**, to cleanse it: after the end of seven months shall they search.*

*Amo 9:6 It is he that buildeth his stories in the heaven, and hath founded his troop in the Earth; he that calleth for the waters of the sea, and poureth them out upon the **face of the Earth**: The LORD is his name.*
*Amo 9:8 Behold, the eyes of the Lord GOD are upon the sinful kingdom, and I will destroy it from off the **face of the Earth**; saving that I will not utterly destroy the house of Jacob, saith the LORD.*

*Zec 5:3 Then said he unto me, This is the curse that goeth forth over the **face of the whole Earth**: for every one that stealeth shall be cut off as on this side according to it; and every one that sweareth shall be cut off as on that side according to it*

*Luk 12:56 Ye hypocrites, ye can discern the **face of the sky and of the Earth;** but how is it that ye do not discern this time?*

*Luk 21:35 For as a snare shall it come on all them that dwell on the **face of the whole Earth**.*

Waters have a Face or a flat Geometrical Surface

Gen 1:2 And the Earth was without form, and void; and darkness was upon the face of the deep. And the Spirit of God moved upon the face of the waters.

Genesis 1:2 describes the Earth as being "without form, and void" with darkness upon the face of the deep and the Spirit of God moving over the face of the waters. From a Flat Earth perspective, the deep refers to the vast waters that surround the Earth rather than empty space. The face of the deep suggests a great flat expanse of water.

This supports the Flat Earth model, where the Earth is surrounded by waters below and above and not floating in the void of empty space. This water is kept from pouring in by the installment of the firmament.

Gen 7:18 And the waters prevailed, and were increased greatly upon the Earth; and the ark went upon the face of the waters.

Genesis 7:18 describes how the floodwaters "prevailed" and "increased greatly upon the Earth," causing the ark to float on the face of the waters. This verse can be understood with an emphasis on the windows of heaven in the firmament opening, allowing the floodwaters to pour onto the Earth.

In this interpretation, the firmament, described as a solid dome separating the waters above from the Earth, opened its windows to release the waters that contributed to the Great Flood. As these waters increased, they covered the Earth, confirming the role of the firmament in holding back vast amounts of water that God released during this catastrophic event. The face of the waters reinforces the idea of a flat surface upon which the ark floated, aligning with the view of a Flat Earth covered by a vast, uniform flood.

Job 38:30 The waters are hid as with a stone, and the face of the deep is frozen.

I believe that in this verse, the waters that are being referred to as being hidden, as with a stone, are the waters that are under the Earth and part of the great deep. These waters are being hidden by the land mass of Earth itself. It also refers to the face of the deep being frozen. This could mean that it is actually frozen like ice or that it is very still, as mentioned in Rev 4:6, which is referred to as a sea of glass-like crystal.

Waters are Straight, not Curved

Job 37:10 By the breath of God frost is given: and the breadth of the waters is straitened.

In Job 37:10, "By the breath of God, frost is given: and the breadth of the waters is straitened," the verse emphasizes God's control over nature, particularly water, and its behavior. Flat Earth believers interpret the "straitening" or stillness of the waters as an indication that water, when undisturbed, naturally settles flat and level. Everyone knows this is true, and it can be demonstrated by anyone.

This fits with the Flat Earth belief that water always finds its level, further supporting the idea that the Earth is flat and not curved, as it would not hold water level if it were a globe. From this perspective, this verse highlights the natural properties of water as evidence of a flat, level Earth.

The Sky has a Face or a Flat Geometrical Surface

Mat 16:3 And in the morning, It will be foul weather to day: for the sky is red and lowring. O ye hypocrites, ye can discern the face of the sky; but can ye not discern the signs of the times?

Luk 12:56 Ye hypocrites, ye can discern the face of the sky and of the Earth; but how is it that ye do not discern this time?

In Matthew 16:3 and Luke 12:56, Jesus refers to the "face of the sky" and the "face of the sky and of the Earth," using the term "face" to describe these expanses. From a Flat Earth perspective, the sky is understood as having a smooth, level surface like a flat face, further supporting the idea of a geometrically Flat Earth.

The use of "face" in these verses implies that both the sky and Earth are perceived as flat surfaces. Just as people can discern the "face" of the sky by observing weather patterns, these verses metaphorically highlight the flat and observable nature of the Earth and heavens, aligning with the belief in a structured, Flat Earth.

The Earth has Ends

The verses from the Bible referencing the ends of the Earth collectively emphasize the vastness of God's dominion and His interaction with creation, suggesting a Flat Earth perspective. The consistent mention of "ends" signifies boundaries that can be perceived as a flat surface rather than a spherical one. On a sphere, one could travel and never reach an end.

Deuteronomy 28:49, 64, 33:17 speaks of nations coming from the ends of the Earth and being scattered among peoples, implying a defined limit that is more easily conceptualized on a flat plane.

Job 38:13 and Psalm 19:4 reference God's reach to the ends of the Earth, portraying a vision of expansiveness that aligns with a flat, extensive surface rather than a curved globe.

Isaiah 40:28 and Isaiah 45:22 highlight God as the creator of the ends of the Earth, reinforcing the notion of a Flat Earth with clearly defined boundaries.

Jeremiah 10:13 and Jeremiah 25:31 express God's authority from the ends of the Earth, indicating that the concept of "end" suggests a flat landscape.

Matthew 12:42 and Luke 11:31 reflect on distant travels to the ends of the Earth, which can be interpreted as journeys across a flat surface rather than around a globe.

These references to the"ends of the Earth"not only illustrate God's sovereignty and the spread of His influence but also invite a reconsideration of how we perceive the Earth's structure, indicating that these descriptions align more naturally with a Flat Earth model rather than a spherical one. This interpretation challenges conventional understandings and encourages deeper reflection on the nature of our world.

The following verses found in the Bible all mention the ends of the Earth:

*Deu 28:49 The LORD shall bring a nation against thee from far, from the **end of the Earth**, as swift as the eagle flieth; a nation whose tongue thou shalt not understand;*

*Deu 28:64 And the LORD shall scatter thee among all people, from the one **end of the Earth** even unto the other; and there thou shalt serve other gods, which neither thou nor thy fathers have known, even wood and stone.*

*Deu 33:17 His glory is like the firstling of his bullock, and his horns are like the horns of unicorns: with them he shall push the people together to the **ends of the Earth**: and they are the ten thousands of Ephraim, and they are the thousands of Manasseh.*

*1Sa 2:10 The adversaries of the LORD shall be broken to pieces; out of heaven shall he thunder upon them: the LORD shall judge **the ends of the Earth**; and he shall give strength unto his king, and exalt the horn of his anointed.*

*Job 28:24 For he looketh to the **ends of the Earth**, and seeth under the whole heaven;*

*Job 37:3 He directeth it under the whole heaven, and his lightning unto the **ends of the Earth**.*

*Job 38:13 That it might take hold of the **ends of the Earth**, that the wicked might be shaken out of it?*

*Psa 19:4 Their line is gone out through all the Earth, and their words to the **end of the world**. In them hath he set a tabernacle for the Sun,*

*Psa 46:9 He maketh wars to cease unto the **end of the Earth**; he breaketh the bow, and cutteth the spear in Sunder; he burneth the chariot in the fire.*

*Psa 48:10 According to thy name, O God, so is thy praise unto the **ends of the Earth**: thy right hand is full of righteousnes.*

*Psa 59:13 Consume them in wrath, consume them, that they may not be: and let them know that God ruleth in Jacob unto the **ends of the Earth**. Selah.*

*Psa 61:2 From the **end of the Earth** will I cry unto thee, when my heart is overwhelmed: lead me to the rock that is higher than I.*

*Psa 65:5 By terrible things in righteousness wilt thou answer us, O God of our salvation; who art the confidence of all the **ends of the Earth**, and of them that are afar off upon the sea:*

*Psa 67:7 God shall bless us; and all the **ends of the Earth** shall fear him.*

*Psa 72:8 He shall have dominion also from sea to sea, and from the river unto the **ends of the Earth**.*

*Psa 98:3 He hath remembered his mercy and his truth toward the house of Israel: all the **ends of the Earth** have seen the salvation of our God.*

*Psa 135:7 He causeth the vapours to ascend from the **ends of the Earth**; he maketh lightnings for the rain; he bringeth the wind out of his treasuries.*

*Pro 17:24 Wisdom is before him that hath understanding; but the eyes of a fool are in the **ends of the Earth**.*

*Pro 30:4 Who hath ascended up into heaven, or descended? who hath gathered the wind in his fists? who hath bound the waters in a garment? who hath established all the **ends of the Earth**? what is his name, and what is his son's name, if thou canst tell?*

*Isa 5:26 And he will lift up an ensign to the nations from far, and will hiss unto them from the **end of the Earth**: and, behold, they shall come with speed swiftly*

*Isa 26:15 Thou hast increased the nation, O LORD, thou hast increased the nation: thou art glorified: thou hadst removed it far unto all the **ends of the Earth**.*

*Isa 40:28 Hast thou not known? hast thou not heard, that the everlasting God, the LORD, the Creator of the **ends of the Earth**, fainteth not, neither is weary? there is no searching of his understanding.*

*Isa 41:5 The isles saw it, and feared; the **ends of the Earth** were afraid, drew near, and came.*

*Isa 41:9 Thou whom I have taken from the **ends of the Earth**, and called thee from the chief men thereof, and said unto thee, Thou art my servant; I have chosen thee, and not cast thee away.*

*Isa 42:10 Sing unto the LORD a new song, and his praise from the **end of the Earth**, ye that go down to the sea, and all that is therein; the isles, and the inhabitants thereof.*

*Isa 43:6 I will say to the north, Give up; and to the south, Keep not back: bring my sons from far, and my daughters from the **ends of the Earth**;*

*Isa 45:22 Look unto me, and be ye saved, all the **ends of the Earth**: for I am God, and there is none else.*

*Isa 48:20 Go ye forth of Babylon, flee ye from the Chaldeans, with a voice of singing declare ye, tell this, utter it even to the **end of the Earth;** say ye, The LORD hath redeemed his servant Jacob*

*Isa 49:6 And he said, It is a light thing that thou shouldest be my servant to raise up the tribes of Jacob, and to restore the preserved of Israel: I will also give thee for a light to the Gentiles, that thou mayest be my salvation unto the **end of the Earth.***

*Isa 52:10 The LORD hath made bare his holy arm in the eyes of all the nations; and all the **ends of the Earth** shall see the salvation of our God.*

*Jer 10:13 When he uttereth his voice, there is a multitude of waters in the heavens, and he causeth the vapours to ascend from the **ends of the Earth**; he maketh lightnings with rain, and bringeth forth the wind out of his treasures.*

*Jer 16:19 O LORD, my strength, and my fortress, and my refuge in the day of affliction, the Gentiles shall come unto thee from the **ends of the Earth**, and shall say, Surely our fathers have inherited lies, vanity, and things wherein there is no profit.*

*Jer 25:31 A noise shall come even to the **ends of the Earth**; for the LORD hath a controversy with the nations, he will plead with all flesh; he will give them that are wicked to the sword, saith the LORD.*

*Jer 25:33 And the slain of the LORD shall be at that day from **one end of the Earth even unto the other end of the Earth**: they shall not be lamented, neither gathered, nor buried; they shall be dung upon the ground.*

*Jer 51:16 When he uttereth his voice, there is a multitude of waters in the heavens; and he causeth the vapours to ascend from the **ends of the Earth**: he maketh lightnings with rain, and bringeth forth the wind out of his treasures.*

*Dan 4:22 It is thou, O king, that art grown and become strong: for thy greatness is grown, and reacheth unto heaven, and thy dominion to the **end of the Earth**.*

*Mic 5:4 And he shall stand and feed in the strength of the LORD, in the majesty of the name of the LORD his God; and they shall abide: for now shall he be great unto the **ends of the Earth**.*

*Zec 9:10 And I will cut off the chariot from Ephraim, and the horse from Jerusalem, and the battle bow shall be cut off: and he shall speak peace unto the heathen: and his dominion shall be from sea even to sea, and from the river even to the **ends of the Earth**.*

*Mat 12:42 The queen of the south shall rise up in the judgment with this generation, and shall condemn it: for she came from **the uttermost parts of the Earth** to hear the wisdom of Solomon; and, behold, a greater than Solomon is here.*

*Luk 11:31 The queen of the south shall rise up in the judgment with the men of this generation, and condemn them: for she came from **the utmost parts of the Earth** to hear the wisdom of Solomon; and, behold, a greater than Solomon is here.*

*Act 13:47 For so hath the Lord commanded us, saying, I have set thee to be a light of the Gentiles, that thou shouldest be for salvation unto the **ends of the Earth**.*

The Earth has Four Corners or Quarters

*Isa 11:12 And he shall set up an ensign for the nations, and shall assemble the outcasts of Israel, and gather together the dispersed of Judah from the **four corners of** the Earth.*

This verse emphasizes the concept of four corners of the Earth, which can be interpreted as a significant indicator of a Flat Earth model. The mention of "four corners" suggests a geometric structure rather than a spherical one, implying distinct boundaries or edges. In the context of Flat Earth theory, this phrase supports the idea of a flat, expansive surface with defined limits, as opposed to a round globe. The imagery of gathering from the four corners reinforces the notion that the Earth has identifiable regions, making it more accessible to understand and navigate, consistent with the Flat Earth perspective.

*Jer 9:26 Egypt, and Judah, and Edom, and the children of Ammon, and Moab, and all that are in the **utmost corners**, that dwell in the wilderness: for all these nations are uncircumcised, and all the house of Israel are uncircumcised in the heart*

*Jer 25:23 Dedan, and Tema, and Buz, and all that are in the **utmost corners**,*

*Ezk 7:2 Also, thou son of man, thus saith the Lord GOD unto the land of Israel; An end, the end is come upon the **four corners** of the land.*

*Rev 7:1 And after these things I saw four angels standing on the **four corners** of the Earth, holding the four winds of the Earth, that the wind should not blow on the Earth, nor on the sea, nor on any tree*

The mention of "four corners of the Earth" implies a geometric structure that can be associated with a Flat Earth model. This description suggests a defined boundary or edge, where each corner represents a distinct point, emphasizing the concept of the Earth having a flat shape rather than a spherical one.

This verse also depicts four angels stationed at these corners, actively restraining the winds from blowing on the Earth, sea, or trees. In a Flat Earth context, this imagery supports the idea that wind patterns can be localized and controlled rather than being subject to the complexities of a spherical atmosphere. The angels' ability to hold back the winds suggests that there are mechanisms—potentially divine or structural— within a Flat Earth framework that manage air currents.
The control over the winds illustrates the power of divine authority and also indicates that the natural elements can be governed in a straightforward manner on a flat surface. If the Earth is flat, the

mechanisms for wind circulation and control become more understandable and accessible, as they are confined to a defined area with clearly defined corners.

*Rev 20:8 And shall go out to deceive the nations which are in the **four quarters** of the Earth, Gog and Magog, to gather them together to battle: the number of whom is as the sand of the sea.*

The phrase "four quarters of the Earth" suggests a divided, flat surface, emphasizing a structured, flat layout rather than a spherical one. This idea resonates with the Flat Earth model, where each quarter can represent distinct geographical or cultural regions, allowing for a clear delineation of areas where Biblical events can unfold.

The gathering of these nations "to battle" indicates a significant war among these nations, each coming from their respective quarters. In a Flat Earth model, this scenario suggests that these nations can assemble more easily and visibly across a unified landscape, reinforcing the idea of a flat quartered plane.

The Wind has a Circuit

*Ecc 1:6 The wind goeth toward the south, and turneth about unto the north; it whirleth about continually, and the wind returneth again according to **his circuits**.*

Ecc 1:6 implies that the behavior of the wind is not random but follows a systematic cycle, which can be compared to weather phenomena observed on a Flat Earth. For example, the patterns of storms, trade winds, and seasonal changes can be visualized more clearly in a model where the Earth is flat, as these patterns would adhere to the flat layout rather than bending around a sphere.

The Earth has Foundations

*Job 38:4 Where wast thou when I laid **the foundations** of the Earth? declare, if thou hast understanding.*

This is one of my favorite verses due to the fact God is asking Job where he was when God laid out the foundations of the Earth. How dare man question God about his perfect creation?

In Job 38:4, God challenges Job, asking where he was when the foundations of the Earth were laid. This verse emphasizes the idea that the Earth has solid, established foundations as if it were built with a purposeful and fixed design. The term "foundations" suggests stability and intentionality, aligning with the Flat Earth theory's belief in a stationary, immovable plane. The verse reinforces the idea that the Earth was carefully and deliberately created, inviting reflection on the nature of its formation and structure. This verse also highlights that man was nowhere around when God laid these foundations and is ignorant of the process involved. Current scientists claim to have all of the answers to how the Earth was formed. The current scientists disregard the creation theory for their satanic Big Bang.

*Job 38:5 Who hath **laid the measures thereof**, if thou knowest? or who hath stretched the line upon it?*

In Job 38:5, God asks who laid the measurements of the Earth or stretched the line upon it, highlighting the mystery of the Earth's dimensions. This verse suggests that the true nature and measurement of the Earth remain beyond human understanding. The "stretching of the line" could be seen as a reference to the Flat Earth's plane being measured out. The verse emphasizes the idea that no human can accurately measure or fully comprehend the vastness and complexity of the Earth, reinforcing the belief in its divine creation and design. I don't think a man could measure it then, and I don't believe scientists can accurately measure it now.

*Job 38:6 Whereupon are **the foundations** thereof fastened? or who laid **the cornerstone** thereof*

In Job 38:6, God asks where the foundations of the Earth are fastened and who laid its cornerstone, pointing to the profound mystery of the Earth's structure. This question emphasizes that no one truly knows the exact nature of the Earth's foundations. The idea of "foundations" and a "cornerstone" suggests a stable, fixed structure, inviting the idea that the Earth is set on a solid, unmoving base and further questioning any claims of knowing exactly how or where these foundations are established. It challenges the heliocentric understanding of the Earth's design.

The following verses also contain the mention of the foundations of the Earth. Some of these verses are listed but not explained in detail. They, like many others, are listed to show you that this is a recurring theme in the Bible. These are not a one-time mention thing.

*Psa 82:5 They know not, neither will they understand; they walk on in darkness: all the **foundations of the Earth** are out of course.*

*Psa 102:25 Of old hast thou laid the **foundation of the Earth**: and the heavens are the work of thy hands.*

*Psa 104:5 Who laid the **foundations of the Earth**, that it should not be removed for ever.*

*Pro 8:29 When he gave to the sea his decree, that the waters should not pass his commandment: when he appointed the **foundations of the Earth***

*Isa 24:18 And it shall come to pass, that he who fleeth from the noise of the fear shall fall into the pit; and he that cometh up out of the midst of the pit shall be taken in the snare: for the windows from on high are open, and the **foundations of the Earth** do shake.*

*Isa 40:21 Have ye not known? have ye not heard? hath it not been told you from the beginning? have ye not understood from the **foundations of the Earth**?*

*Isa 48:13 Mine hand also hath laid the **foundation of the Earth**, and my right hand hath spanned the heavens: when I call unto them, they stand up together.*

*Isa 51:13 And forgettest the LORD thy maker, that hath stretched forth the heavens, and laid the **foundations of the Earth**; and hast feared continually every day because of the fury of the oppressor, as if he were ready to destroy? and where is the fury of the oppressor?*

*Isa 51:16 And I have put my words in thy mouth, and I have covered thee in the shadow of mine hand, that I may plant the heavens, and lay the **foundations of the Earth**, and say unto Zion, Thou art my people.*

*Mic 6:2 Hear ye, O mountains, the LORD'S controversy, and ye **strong foundations of the Earth**: for the LORD hath a controversy with his people, and he will plead with Israel.*

*Zec 12:1 The burden of the word of the LORD for Israel, saith the LORD, which stretcheth forth the heavens, and layeth the **foundation of the Earth**, and formeth the spirit of man within him.*

*Heb 1:10 And, Thou, Lord, in the beginning hast laid the **foundation of the Earth**; and the heavens are the works of thine hands:*

Common sense would tell you that the laying of any foundation has to be strong and level to support a structure that is placed above the foundation. It only stands to reason that this is how the Earth's foundation was laid as well.

The Earth has Pillars

*1Sa 2:8 He raiseth up the poor out of the dust, and lifteth up the beggar from the dunghill, to set them among princes, and to make them inherit the throne of glory: for **the pillars of the Earth** are the LORD'S, and he hath set the world upon them.*

In 1 Samuel 2:8, it is stated that "the pillars of the Earth are the LORD'S, and he hath set the world upon them." This verse, along with others that reference the pillars of the Earth (such as Job 9:6 and Psalm 75:3), emphasizes the concept of the Earth being upheld by firm, immovable pillars. This imagery supports the belief that the Earth is not suspended in space but rests on a stable, foundational structure. The idea of pillars suggests a flat, fixed Earth, grounded on solid supports, rather than a spinning globe suspended in space, reinforcing the view that the Earth is stable and unmovable under God's design. This understanding ties into the Flat Earth theory by portraying the Earth as a flat plane supported by divine foundations.

*Job 9:6 Which shaketh the Earth out of her place, and the **pillars** thereof tremble.*

*Psa 75:3 The Earth and all the inhabitants thereof are dissolved: I bear up the **pillars** of it. Selah*

The Earth is Fixed and Immovable

In Psalm 93:1, it says, "The world also is established, that it cannot be moved." This, along with verses like 1 Chronicles 16:30 ("the world also shall be stable, that it be not moved") and Psalm 104:5 ("Who laid the foundations of the Earth, that it should not be removed forever"), suggests a clear biblical perspective that the Earth is stable and immovable. These verses are interpreted by Flat Earth theorists to support the idea that the Earth is not spinning or moving through space. Instead, we argue that the Bible describes the Earth as a fixed, stable plane, firmly set in place by God, unmoved by external forces, which contrasts with the scientific view of a rotating globe in space. This biblical foundation serves to reinforce the Flat Earth model, where the Earth remains motionless beneath a firmament.

1Ch 16:30 Fear before him, all the Earth: the world also shall be stable, **that it be not moved**.

*Psa 33:9 For he spake, and it was done; he commanded, and **it stood fast**.*

*Psa 93:1 The LORD reigneth, he is clothed with majesty; the LORD is clothed with strength, wherewith he hath girded himself: the world also is stablished, **that it cannot be moved**.*

*Psa 96:10 Say among the heathen that the LORD reigneth: the world also shall be established that it **shall not be moved**: he shall judge the people righteously.*

*Psa 104:5 Who laid the foundations of the Earth, that it **should not be removed** for ever.*

*Isa 14:7 The whole **Earth is at rest,** and is quiet: they break forth into singing.*

*Zec 1:11 And they answered the angel of the LORD that stood among the myrtle trees, and said, We have walked to and fro through the Earth, and, behold, all the **Earth sitteth still, and is at rest**.*

The Earth is Surrounded by Water

*2Pe 3:5 For this they willingly are ignorant of, that by the word of God the heavens were of old, and the **Earth standing out of the water and in the water:***

In this verse, Peter talks about people being willingly ignorant of certain Biblical facts. One of the things that he mentions is that the Earth stands out of the water and in the water. This perfectly describes the Flat Earth that is situated under the dome of the firmament. In this enclosed system, there is the water of great deep that surrounds the Earth as we know it. We have the Earth standing out of the water of the seas that are under the firmament, and we have the Earth standing in the water of the deep, protected by the firmament.

Does an Ice Wall Surround the Oceans?

*Job 26:10 He hath **compassed the waters with bounds**, until the day and night come to an end.*

Job 26:10 describes God as having "compassed the waters with bounds until the day and night come to an end." Flat Earth proponents interpret this as referring to the waters of the Earth being enclosed by an ice wall or the Antarctic Circle, which acts as a boundary for the oceans. This interpretation suggests that the Earth is surrounded by a barrier that holds the waters in place, supporting the idea of a Flat Earth with the Antarctic ice wall marking the edge. The verse emphasizes the fixed nature of these bounds, lasting until the end of time.

At this time, it is unknown what is beyond this ice wall barrier. This verse shows that the waters of the Earth are not just held to the Earth by a magical force called gravity, but have a boundary set by God.

Earth Compared to a Flattened-out Seal with Upturned Edges

*Job 38:14 It is **turned as clay to the seal**; and they stand as a garment.*

In Job 38:14, the verse says, "It is turned as clay to the seal, and they stand as a garment." In the context of Flat Earth theory, this verse can be interpreted to suggest that the Earth has a shape similar to a wax seal. A wax seal, when pressed by a signet ring, creates a flat surface with upturned edges. This imagery is used by Flat Earth proponents to describe the Earth as being flat with raised edges. This raised edge is compared to how the Antarctic ice wall is raised above all other land masses.

The verse's comparison of the Earth to a wax seal can be seen as emphasizing the flat, level surface of the Earth, while the "upturned edges" relate to the boundary of the ice wall that encircles and contains the seas. The Earth is similarly flat and contained.

The Oceans are Fed Water

From the Great Deep

*Job 38:16 Hast thou entered into the **springs of the sea**? or hast thou walked in the search of the depth?*

This verse can be interpreted to suggest that the oceans are fed by springs from the "great deep" beneath the Earth.

This interpretation proposes that these underground springs control the ocean's tides and water flow, challenging the conventional idea of the Moon's role in tidal movements. The verse highlights the mysterious nature of the deep waters and suggests that the water outside the firmament feeds these springs. The tides are certainly not caused by the sloshing of the oceans, like Galileo claimed.

The Earth is God's Footstool

*Isa 66:1 Thus saith the LORD, The heaven is my throne, and **the Earth is my footstool**: where is the house that ye build unto me? and where is the place of my rest?*

Isaiah 66:1 emphasizes that God is in heaven, sitting on His throne, while the Earth is described as His footstool. This suggests that the Earth holds a special place in creation and is the center of that creation. The idea that the Earth is His footstool can be interpreted to mean that the Earth is central to God's creation and His plan. From this perspective, the Earth is not only under divine watch but also holds unique importance as the place where humanity resides and where God's presence can be felt, aligning with a view of the Earth as the centerpiece of creation.

*Mat 5:35 Nor by the **Earth; for it is his footstool**: neither by Jerusalem; for it is the city of the great King.*

Kenny Williamson

The Sun Moved Backward

In 2 Kings 20:8-11, King Hezekiah asks for a sign from the Lord to confirm that he will be healed. Isaiah, the prophet, offers Hezekiah a miraculous sign involving the movement of the Sun's shadow. Hezekiah chooses for the shadow to move backward ten degrees, which the Lord miraculously accomplishes. This event demonstrates that the Sun itself moved, causing the shadow to reverse on the Sundial. From the perspective of a Flat Earth theory, this proves that the Sun moves around the Earth, rather than the Earth revolving around the Sun, as the Sun's motion is directly altered in this account, affirming geocentrism.

2Ki 20:8 And Hezekiah said unto Isaiah, What shall be the sign that the LORD will heal me, and that I shall go up into the house of the LORD the third day?

2Ki 20:9 And Isaiah said, This sign shalt thou have of the LORD, that the LORD will do the thing that he hath spoken: shall the shadow go forward ten degrees, or go back ten degrees?

2Ki 20:10 And Hezekiah answered, It is a light thing for the shadow to go down ten degrees: nay, but let the shadow return backward ten degrees.

2Ki 20:11 And Isaiah the prophet cried unto the LORD: and he brought the shadow ten degrees backward, by which it had gone down in the dial of Ahaz

Kenny Williamson

The Sun and Moon Stop Moving

In Joshua 10:12-13, Joshua prays to the Lord during a battle, asking
for the Sun and Moon to stand still. God miraculously answers,
causing the Sun to stop over Gibeon and the Moon to pause over the
valley of Ajalon, halting their movement until Israel achieves victory.
From a Flat Earth perspective, this passage emphasizes that the Sun
and Moon move around the Earth, not the other way around. The
halting of both the Sun and Moon proves that they are independent
lights traveling across the sky, reinforcing a geocentric model where
the Earth remains stationary, and the celestial bodies move around it.

*Jos 10:12 Then spake Joshua to the LORD in the day when the LORD
delivered up the Amorites before the children of Israel, and he said in
the sight of Israel,* **Sun, stand thou still** *upon Gibeon; and thou, Moon,
in the valley of Ajalon.*

Jos 10:13 **And the Sun stood still, and the Moon stayed,** *until the
people had avenged themselves upon their enemies. Is not this written
in the book of Jasher? So the Sun stood still in the midst of heaven,
and hasted not to go down about a whole day.*

In Job 9:7, it is said that God has the power to command the Sun not to
rise and to seal up the stars. This emphasizes God's supreme control
over the heavens and the celestial bodies. From a Flat Earth

perspective, this could be seen as further evidence that the Sun is not a fixed object that the Earth revolves around, but rather something that God can command to stop its movement, supporting the idea that the Sun moves over a stationary, Flat Earth. The stars being "sealed up" also points to God's control over the firmament and the celestial lights within it.

Job 9:7 Which commandeth the Sun, and it riseth not; and sealeth up the stars.

In Habakkuk 3:11, it is described that the Sun and Moon stood still in their habitation, pausing in response to God's mighty power. From a Flat Earth perspective, this verse could be interpreted to mean that the Sun and Moon, which are viewed as moving over the Earth, can be halted by divine command. Their "habitation" could suggest fixed paths in the sky, further supporting the belief that they move in circuits above a stationary, Flat Earth rather than the Earth moving around them. This emphasizes God's authority over the celestial bodies.

*Hab 3:11 The **Sun and Moon stood still in their habitation**: at the light of thine arrows they went, and at the shining of thy glittering spear.*

The Moon is its Own Light

The Bible contains several verses that refer to the Moon as "her" and describe it as a source of its own light. One key verse is Isaiah 13:10, which says, "For the stars of heaven and their constellations will not give their light; the Sun will be darkened in its going forth, and the Moon will not cause her light to shine." This verse, along with others like Mark 13:24 and Matthew 24:29, refers to the Moon as "her," indicating a feminine personification.

Additionally, in Genesis 1:16, the Bible describes the Moon as the "lesser light to rule the night," which suggests that the Moon has its own light rather than merely reflecting Sunlight. From a Flat Earth perspective, these verses can be interpreted to mean that the Moon is not just a reflector of the Sun's light but a luminary in its own right, shining its own light to rule the night. This challenges the modern scientific understanding of the Moon reflecting the Sun's light, reinforcing the idea of the Moon as an independent light source.

Gen 1:16 And God made two great lights; the greater light to rule the day, and the lesser light to rule the night: he made the stars also

Isa 13:10 For the stars of heaven and the constellations thereof shall not give their light: the Sun shall be darkened in his going forth, and the Moon shall not cause her light to shine.

Isa 30:26 Moreover the light of the Moon shall be as the light of the Sun, and the light of the Sun shall be sevenfold, as the light of seven days, in the day that the LORD bindeth up the breach of his people, and healeth the stroke of their wound.

Jer 31:35 Thus saith the LORD, which giveth the Sun for a light by day, and the ordinances of the Moon and of the stars for a light by night, which divideth the sea when the waves thereof roar; The LORD of hosts is his name:

Ezk 32:7 And when I shall put thee out, I will cover the heaven, and make the stars thereof dark; I will cover the Sun with a cloud, and the Moon shall not give her light.

Mat 24:29 Immediately after the tribulation of those days shall the Sun be darkened, and the Moon shall not give her light, and the stars shall fall from heaven, and the powers of the heavens shall be shaken:

Mrk 13:24 But in those days, after that tribulation, the Sun shall be darkened, and the Moon shall not give her light,

Creation Worshipers

These following verses speak clearly about the dangers of worshiping celestial bodies—such as the Sun, Moon, stars, and planets—rather than worshiping God, who created these objects. In Deuteronomy 4:19, the warning is given not to look up at the heavens and be tempted to worship the Sun, Moon, and stars, even though God divided them into all nations. Deuteronomy 17:3 reiterates this warning, condemning the worship of the Sun, Moon, or any host of heaven as idolatry, which God has not commanded. 2 Kings 23:5 tells of King Josiah's reforms, where he abolished the idolatrous worship of these celestial bodies, showing that even in Israel, people had been led astray to worship creation rather than the Creator. Jeremiah 8:2 warns that those who worshiped the Sun, Moon, and stars will be humiliated and reduced to nothing more than dung upon the Earth.

In Acts 14:11-12, we see how quickly people can fall into creation worship and idolatry when the crowd mistook Paul and Barnabas for gods, associating them with the planets Jupiter and Mercury. This reflects the persistent human tendency to worship aspects of creation rather than the one true God.

Relating this to the modern world, many people today are fascinated by space and outer space exploration, often focusing on the grandeur of the universe and celestial bodies, which can be seen as a modern form of creation worship. In some cases, pursuing knowledge about the universe becomes an obsession, drawing attention away from the Creator and turning the focus toward what has been created. From a biblical perspective, this is akin to the idolatry condemned in these verses. God desires that people worship Him alone and not be distracted or deceived by the wonders of the heavens, whether through ancient idolatry or modern fascination with "outer space."

Deu 4:19 And lest thou lift up thine eyes unto heaven, and when thou seest the Sun, and the Moon, and the stars, even all the host of heaven, shouldest be driven to worship them, and serve them, which the LORD thy God hath divided unto all nations under the whole heaven.

Deu 17:3 And hath gone and served other gods, and worshipped them, either the Sun, or Moon, or any of the host of heaven, which I have not commanded;

2Ki 23:5 And he put down the idolatrous priests, whom the kings of Judah had ordained to burn incense in the high places in the cities of Judah, and in the places round about Jerusalem; them also that burned incense unto Baal, to the Sun, and to the Moon, and to the planets, and to all the host of heaven.

Jer 8:2 And they shall spread them before the Sun, and the Moon, and all the host of heaven, whom they have loved, and whom they have served, and after whom they have walked, and whom they have sought, and whom they have worshipped: they shall not be gathered, nor be buried; they shall be for dung upon the face of the Earth.

Act 14:11 And when the people saw what Paul had done, they lifted up their voices, saying in the speech of Lycaonia, The gods are come down to us in the likeness of men.

Act 14:12 And they called Barnabas, Jupiter; and Paul, Mercurius, because he was the chief speaker.

The Sun Moves, Not the Earth

Throughout the Bible, verses often describe the Sun as rising, setting, or moving in its course, portraying it as an object in motion rather than the Earth. In Genesis, the story of creation describes God placing the Sun in the sky to govern the day and states it rises and sets. Ecclesiastes 1:5 also reflects this, saying, "The Sun also ariseth, and the Sun goeth down, and hasteth to his place where he arose, "indicating a cycle of movement specifically attributed to the Sun.

In Psalm 113:3, the psalmist writes, "From the rising of the Sun unto the going down of the same, the LORD's name is to be praised," showing that the Sun's predictable rising and setting are understood as movements of the Sun, not of the Earth. Joshua 10:13 offers a similar picture when God made the Sun "stand still" at Joshua's request, stopping it in the sky to allow victory in battle. If the Earth were rotating around the Sun, such an act would seem irrelevant, but in a Flat Earth view, this verse proves the idea that the Sun moves over the Earth.

These verses emphasize the Sun's motion, implying a stationary Earth beneath it, which aligns with the Flat Earth model's view of the Earth as stable and immovable, with the Sun moving over it in a predictable path. This concept is repeatedly used to mark time and seasons and reinforces a view of the Earth as the fixed center of God's creation, with celestial bodies moving over it as part of a purposeful design.

*Gen 15:12 And when the **Sun was going down**, a deep sleep fell upon Abram; and, lo, an horror of great darkness fell upon him.*

*Gen 15:17 And it came to pass, that, when the **Sun went down**, and it was dark, behold a smoking furnace, and a burning lamp that passed between those pieces.*

*Gen 19:23 The **Sun was risen** upon the Earth when Lot entered into Zoar.*

*Gen 32:31 And as he passed over Penuel the **Sun rose** upon him, and he halted upon his thigh.*

*Exo 17:12 But Moses' hands were heavy; and they took a stone, and put it under him, and he sat thereon; and Aaron and Hur stayed up his hands, the one on the one side, and the other on the other side; and his hands were steady until the **going down of the Sun**.*

*Exo 22:3 If the **Sun be risen** upon him, there shall be blood shed for him; for he should make full restitution; if he have nothing, then he shall be sold for his theft*

*Exo 22:26 If thou at all take thy neighbour's raiment to pledge, thou shalt deliver it unto him by that the **Sun goeth down**:*

*Lev 22:7 And when the **Sun is down**, he shall be clean, and shall afterward eat of the holy things; because it is his food.*

*Num 2:3 And, on the east side toward the **rising of the Sun** shall they of the standard of the camp of Judah pitch throughout their armies: and Nahshon the son of Amminadab shall be captain of the children of Judah.*

*Num 21:11 And they journeyed from Oboth, and pitched at Ijeabarim, in the wilderness which is before Moab, toward **the Sunrising**.*

*Num 21:11 And they journeyed from Oboth, and pitched at Ijeabarim, in the wilderness which is before Moab, toward **the Sunrising**.*

*Deu 4:41 Then Moses severed three cities on this side Jordan toward **the Sunrising**;*

*Deu 4:47 And they possessed his land, and the land of Og king of Bashan, two kings of the Amorites, which were on this side Jordan toward **the Sunrising**;*

*Deu 11:30 Are they not on the other side Jordan, by the way where the **Sun goeth down**, in the land of the Canaanites, which dwell in the champaign over against Gilgal, beside the plains of Moreh?*

*Deu 16:6 But at the place which the LORD thy God shall choose to place his name in, there thou shalt sacrifice the passover at even, at the **going down of the Sun**, at the season that thou camest forth out of Egypt.*

*Deu 23:11 But it shall be, when evening cometh on, he shall wash himself with water: and when **the Sun is down**, he shall come into the camp again*

*Deu 24:13 In any case thou shalt deliver him the pledge again when the **Sun goeth down**, that he may sleep in his own raiment, and bless thee: and it shall be righteousness unto thee before the LORD thy God.*

*Deu 24:15 At his day thou shalt give him his hire, **neither shall the Sun go down** upon it; for he is poor, and setteth his heart upon it: lest he cry against thee unto the LORD, and it be sin unto thee.*

*Jos 1:15 Until the LORD have given your brethren rest, as he hath given you, and they also have possessed the land which the LORD your God giveth them: then ye shall return unto the land of your possession, and enjoy it, which Moses the LORD'S servant gave you on this side Jordan toward **the Sunrising**.*

*Jos 8:29 And the king of Ai he hanged on a tree until eventide: and as soon as the **Sun was down**, Joshua commanded that they should take his carcase down from the tree, and cast it at the entering of the gate of the city, and raise thereon a great heap of stones, that remaineth unto this day*

*Jos 10:27 And it came to pass at the time of the **going down of the Sun**, that Joshua commanded, and they took them down off the trees, and cast them into the cave wherein they had been hid, and laid great stones in the cave's mouth, which remain until this very day.*

*Jos 12:1 Now these are the kings of the land, which the children of Israel smote, and possessed their land on the other side Jordan toward the **rising of the Sun**, from the river Arnon unto mount Hermon, and all the plain on the east*

*Jos 13:5 And the land of the Giblites, and all Lebanon, toward **the Sunrising**, from Baalgad under mount Hermon unto the entering into Hamath*

*Jos 19:12 And turned from Sarid eastward toward **the Sunrising** unto the border of Chislothtabor, and then goeth out to Daberath, and goeth up to Japhia,*

*Jos 19:27 And turneth toward **the Sunrising** to Bethdagon, and reacheth to Zebulun, and to the valley of Jiphthahel toward the north side of Bethemek, and Neiel, and goeth out to Cabul on the left hand,*

*Jos 19:34 And then the coast turneth westward to Aznothtabor, and goeth out from thence to Hukkok, and reacheth to Zebulun on the south side, and reacheth to Asher on the west side, and to Judah upon Jordan toward **the Sunrising**.*

*Jdg 8:13 And Gideon the son of Joash returned from battle before the **Sun was up***

*Jdg 9:33 And it shall be, that in the morning, as soon as **the Sun is up**, thou shalt rise early, and set upon the city: and, behold, when he* and the people that is with him come out against thee, then mayest thou do to them as thou shalt find occasion

*Jdg 14:18 And the men of the city said unto him on the seventh day before the **Sun went down**, What is sweeter than honey? and what is stronger than a lion? And he said unto them, If ye had not plowed with my heifer, ye had not found out my riddle.*

*Jdg 19:14 And they passed on and went their way; and the **Sun went down** upon them when they were by Gibeah, which belongeth to Benjamin.*

*Jdg 20:43 Thus they inclosed the Benjamites round about, and chased them, and trode them down with ease over against Gibeah toward **the Sunrising**.*

*2Sa 2:24 Joab also and Abishai pursued after Abner: and the **Sun went down** when they were come to the hill of Ammah, that lieth before Giah by the way of the wilderness of Gibeon.*

*2Sa 3:35 And when all the people came to cause David to eat meat while it was yet day, David sware, saying, So do God to me, and more also, if I taste bread, or ought else, till the **Sun be down**.*

*1Ki 22:36 And there went a proclamation throughout the host about the **going down of the Sun**, saying, Every man to his city, and every man to his own country.*

*2Ch 18:34 And the battle increased that day: howbeit the king of Israel stayed himself up in his chariot against the Syrians until the even: and about the time of the **Sun going down** he died.*

*Psa 50:1 A Psalm of Asaph. The mighty God, even the LORD, hath spoken, and called the Earth from the **rising of the Sun** unto the going down thereof.*

*Psa 113:3 From the **rising of the Sun** unto the going down of the same the LORD'S name is to be praised.*

*Ecc 1:5 The **Sun also ariseth**, and the **Sun goeth down**, and **hasteth to his place** where he arose.*

*Isa 41:25 I have raised up one from the north, and he shall come: from the **rising of the Sun** shall he call upon my name: and he shall come upon princes as upon morter, and as the potter treadeth clay.*

*Isa 45:6 That they may know from the **rising of the Sun**, and from the west, that there is none beside me. I am the LORD, and there is none else.*

*Isa 59:19 So shall they fear the name of the LORD from the west, and his glory from the **rising of the Sun**. When the enemy shall come in like a flood, the Spirit of the LORD shall lift up a standard against him.*

*Jer 15:9 She that hath borne seven languisheth: she hath given up the ghost; her **Sun is gone down** while it was yet day: she hath been ashamed and confounded: and the residue of them will I deliver to the sword before their enemies, saith the LORD.*

*Dan 6:14 Then the king, when he heard these words, was sore displeased with himself, and set his heart on Daniel to deliver him: and he laboured till the **going down of the Sun** to deliver him.*

*Amo 8:9 And it shall come to pass in that day, saith the Lord GOD, that I will cause the **Sun to go down at noon**, and I will darken the Earth in the clear day:*

*Jon 4:8 And it came to pass, when **the Sun did arise**, that God prepared a vehement east wind; and the Sun beat upon the head of Jonah, that he fainted, and wished in himself to die, and said, It is better for me to die than to live.*

*Mic 3:6 Therefore night shall be unto you, that ye shall not have a vision; and it shall be dark unto you, that ye shall not divine; and the **Sun shall go down** over the prophets, and the day shall be dark over them.*

*Nah 3:17 Thy crowned are as the locusts, and thy captains as the great grasshoppers, which camp in the hedges in the cold day, but when **the Sun ariseth** they flee away, and their place is not known where they are.*

*Mal 1:11 For from the **rising of the Sun** even unto the going down of the same my name shall be great among the Gentiles; and in every place incense shall be offered unto my name, and a pure offering: for my name shall be great among the heathen, saith the LORD of hosts. Mat 5:45 That ye may be the children of your Father which is in heaven: for he maketh **his Sun to rise** on the evil and on the good, and sendeth rain on the just and on the unjust.*

*Mar 16:2 And very early in the morning the first day of the week, they came unto the sepulchre at the **rising of the Sun**.*

*Eph 4:26 Be ye angry, and sin not: let not the **Sun go down** upon your wrath:*

*Jas 1:11 For the **Sun is no sooner risen** with a burning heat, but it withereth the grass, and the flower thereof falleth, and the grace of the fashion of it perisheth: so also shall the rich man fade away in his ways.*

High Altitude Perspectives

These verses describe elevated perspectives that suggest the possibility of seeing vast areas of the Earth from a high vantage point, aligning with a Flat Earth interpretation. In Daniel 4:11 and 4:20, the imagery of a great tree reaching "unto heaven" with its sight extending "to the end of all the Earth" implies that from a certain height, one could view the entire plane of the Earth under the firmament. This description supports the idea of a flat plane, as only on such a surface could a single point be visible across all the Earth.

Similarly, Matthew 4:8 describes the devil taking Jesus to an "exceeding high mountain," from which he shows him "all the kingdoms of the world." This account suggests that from a high place, it is possible to see all regions of the Earth, again supporting the Flat Earth concept of a vast, level expanse. In these passages, the heavens are understood as the firmament—a boundary above the Earth—and these observations from high altitudes reinforce the view that the Earth's surface is flat, allowing for such complete, unobstructed views.

*Dan 4:11 The tree grew, and was strong, and the height thereof reached unto heaven, and the sight thereof to **the end of all the Earth**:*

*Dan 4:20 The tree that thou sawest, which grew, and was strong, whose height reached unto the heaven, and the sight **thereof to all the Earth;***

*Mat 4:8 Again, the devil taketh him up into an **exceeding high mountain, and sheweth him all the kingdoms of the world,** and the glory of them;*

The Sun Travels in a Circuit

These verses suggest that the Sun follows its own fixed path or "circuit," rising and setting in a repetitive cycle that it hastens to complete each day. For example, Ecclesiastes 1:5 states, "The Sun also rises, and the Sun goes down and hastens to the place where it arose," portraying the Sun as moving independently along a set course. This imagery implies that the Sun itself is moving, not the Earth, as it travels across the sky and returns to its starting point.

This repeated cycle reflects the Flat Earth perspective, where the Sun moves over the Earth in a circuit, creating day and night by moving across a fixed plane. Instead of the Earth rotating around the Sun, the verses imply that the Sun's movement alone generates the day-night sequence, supporting the idea of a stationary Earth under a moving Sun.

Psa 19:4 Their line is gone out through all the Earth, and their words to the end of the world. In them hath he set a tabernacle for the Sun,

Psa 19:5 Which is as a bridegroom coming out of his chamber, and rejoiceth as a strong man to run a race.

Psa 19:6 His going forth is from the end of the heaven, and his circuit unto the ends of it: and there is nothing hid from the heat thereof

Ecc 1:5 The Sun also ariseth, and the Sun goeth down, and hasteth to his place where he arose.

The Bible Clearly teaches that the Sun is moving around the Earth and not the other way around. These verses are not trying to convince you of that fact; they are just describing what they assume you already know. When the Bible was penned, they already knew that the Sun was moving and not the Earth. It is man's new knowlege that is calling God a liar.

The Earth has a Width and a Breadth

The verses mentioning the Earth's "length" and "breadth" suggest that it has defined measurements, like a flat surface that can be walked across and measured. Genesis 13:17 describes God instructing Abraham to walk the land "in the length of it and in the breadth of it," implying that the land's dimensions can be experienced directly by walking across a defined plane.

In Job 38:18, God asks if anyone truly perceives "the breadth of the Earth," suggesting a vast yet measurable span. Likewise, Isaiah 8:8 and Revelation 20:9 both refer to the "breadth" of the Earth, highlighting that the land extends across a broad, spread-out area.

From a Flat Earth perspective, these verses emphasize an Earth with a measurable width and length, a surface more like a vast, spread-out plane than a spherical shape. This understanding aligns with the idea of the Earth as a flat surface that stretches outward in both length and breadth, allowing for a view of its expansive reach.

Gen 13:17 Arise, walk through the land in the length of it and in the **breadth of it**; *for I will give it unto thee.*

Job 38:18 Hast thou perceived the **breadth of the Earth**? *declare if thou knowest it all.*

*Isa 8:8 And he shall pass through Judah; he shall overflow and go over, he shall reach even to the neck; and the stretching out of his wings shall fill **the breadth of thy land**, O Immanuel.*

*Pro 25:3 The heaven for height, and the **Earth for depth**, and the heart of kings is unsearchable.*

*Rev 20:9 And they went up on the **breadth of the Earth**, and compassed the camp of the saints about, and the beloved city: and fire came down from God out of heaven, and devoured them.*

Earth Has an Up and a Down

These verses collectively reinforce the concept of an "up" and "down," showing a clear directionality that contrasts with scientific views of a boundless space where there is no fixed up or down. Deuteronomy 4:39 points to God in "heaven above" and the Earth "beneath," indicating a separation between a higher and lower realm. John 3:13 emphasizes that no one has "ascended up to heaven" except Christ, who descended, showing heaven as a distinctly higher place.

In Acts 1:9-11, Jesus ascends "up" into the sky, where the disciples look steadfastly upward, affirming a universally understood "upward" direction to heaven. Similarly, 1 Thessalonians 4:16-17f speaks of the Lord descending from heaven and the faithful being "caught up" to meet Him in the air, reinforcing this directional view.

From a Flat Earth perspective, these passages depict a structured world with a clear "up" and "down." Rather than a globe floating in space with no directional fixedness, this view supports a Flat Earth with an above (heaven) and hell below, just as people experience intuitively when they look up to the sky. Everyone instinctively knows what up and down is. It is only our current so-called scientists that claim a spinning ball in space has no up or down.

Deu 4:39 Know therefore this day, and consider it in thine heart, that the LORD he is God in heaven above, and upon the Earth beneath: there is none else.

Joh 3:13 And no man hath ascended up to heaven, but he that came down from heaven, even the Son of man which is in heaven.

Act 1:9 And when he had spoken these things, while they beheld, he was taken up; and a cloud received him out of their sight.

Act 1:10 And while they looked stedfastly toward heaven as he went up, behold, two men stood by them in white apparel;

Act 1:11 Which also said, Ye men of Galilee, why stand ye gazing up into heaven? this same Jesus, which is taken up from you into heaven, shall so come in like manner as ye have seen him go into heaven

1Th 4:16 For the Lord himself shall descend from heaven with a shout, with the voice of the archangel, and with the trump of God: and the dead in Christ shall rise first:

1Th 4:17 Then we which are alive and remain shall be caught up together with them in the clouds, to meet the Lord in the air: and so shall we ever be with the Lord.

Everyone Sees Jesus at the Same Time

Revelation 1:7 states, "Behold, he cometh with clouds; and every eye shall see him." This verse emphasizes that when Jesus returns, everyone across the Earth will witness His descent from heaven simultaneously, including those who had a role in His crucifixion and all "kindreds of the Earth." From a Flat Earth perspective, this would be possible because the flat plane allows for an unobstructed view of the sky across all regions.

On a globe, it would be impossible for people on opposite sides of the Earth to see the same event at the exact moment due to the curvature of the Earth. Therefore, I personally see this as direct support for a Flat Earth, where all people on Earth will witness this wonderful event at the same moment in time.

*Rev 1:7 Behold, **he cometh with clouds; and every eye shall see him**, and they also which pierced him: and all kindreds of the Earth shall wail because of him. Even so, Amen.*

The Sun and Moon no longer Shine

In these verses, the idea of God as the ultimate source of light shows us God's eternal perfection, where the Sun and Moon become unnecessary because the divine presence of God fulfills all illumination needs. This also shows that the Earth is not revolving around the Sun, and the Moon is not controlling the tides. They are both acting as light sources that God's light can replace.

In Isaiah 60:19-20, the prophecy speaks to a time when sorrow will end, and God's everlasting light will replace the regular cycles of night and day. This symbolizes peace, eternal life, and the constant presence of God's glory.

Similarly, in Revelation 21:23, the image of the New Jerusalem needing no Sun or Moon emphasizes that God's glory and the presence of the Lamb (Jesus) provide perpetual light in this perfected state. This vision implies that God's presence is so powerful that it sustains all life, joy, and knowledge, rendering Earthly lights obsolete. Together, these verses represent a future where God's presence provides unending light, peace, and fulfillment.

This is another proof that the Earth does not revolve around the Sun. This is hardly what NASA teaches.

Isa 60:20 Thy Sun shall no more go down; neither shall thy Moon withdraw itself: for the LORD shall be thine everlasting light, and the days of thy mourning shall be ended.

Isa 60:19 The Sun shall be no more thy light by day; neither for brightness shall the Moon give light unto thee: but the LORD shall be unto thee an everlasting light, and thy God thy glory.

Rev 21:23 And the city had no need of the Sun, neither of the Moon, to shine in it: for the glory of God did lighten it, and the Lamb is the light thereof

Kenny Williamson

Matthews Bible from 1537

*2 Samuel 11:11 And Vrias sayd vnto Dauid: the arck and Israel & Iuda dwell in pauilions: & my Lord Ioab and the seruauntes of my Lorde lye in tentes **vpon the Flat Earthe**: and shulde I then go into myne house, to eate and to dryncke & to lye wyth my wyfe? By thy lyfe and as sure as thy soule lyueth, I wyll not do that thyng.*

This verse from a pre-KJV Bible suggests a depiction of the "Flat Earth" language in early English translations. In this passage, Uriah speaks to King David, emphasizing his dedication to Israel's military efforts while he refuses to return to his home for comfort.

This Matthews Bible from the year 1537 predates the Authorized Version or the King James Version, which was released in 1611. I only endorse the King James Version, but I wanted to show you that the words "Flat Earth" were actually printed in early Bibles. As you can see in this verse, it is talking about where the tents are being used. This could mean just a small area of flat ground where they are encamped. I have included this verse just for reference only; I believe that there are many verses in the King James Bible that prove that the Earth is not a spinning globe in outer space.

I don't believe that this verse is a smoking gun.

Terra Firma: 1901

"I remember being taught when a boy, that the Earth was a great ball, revolving at a very rapid rate around the Sun, and, when I expressed to my teacher my fears that the waters of the oceans would tumble off, I was told that they were prevented from doing so by Newton's great law of Gravitation, which kept everything in its proper place.

I presume that my countenance must have shown some signs of incredulity, for my teacher immediately added – I can show you direct proof of this; a man can whirl around his head a pail filled with water without its being spilled, and so, in like manner, can the oceans be carried round the Sun without losing a drop. As this illustration was evidently intended to settle the matter, I then said no more upon the subject.

Had such been proposed to me afterward as a man, I would have answered somewhat as follows – Sir, I beg to say that the illustration you have given of a man whirling a pail of water around his head and the oceans revolving around the Sun, does not in any degree confirm your argument, because the water in the two cases is placed under entirely different circumstances, but, to be of any value, the conditions in each case must be the same, which here they are not.

The pail is a hollow vessel which holds the water inside it, whereas, according to your teaching, the Earth is a ball, with a continuous curvature outside, which, in agreement with the laws of nature, could not retain any water."

David Wardlaw Scott, "Terra Firma: The Earth Not a Planet Proved From Scripture, Reason, and Fact"

Acknowledgments

I would like to express my deep gratitude to Jonnie Allan, Joey Faust and David Weiss for their dedication to exploring alternative perspectives on our world. Their thought-provoking work and research have inspired countless individuals to question, explore, and seek knowledge with open minds. Their insights and theories have been invaluable in shaping many ideas presented here, and I am grateful for their contributions to the community of independent researchers and thinkers.

Flat Earth links:

flatearthdave.com

itsflatbro.com

Made in the USA
Columbia, SC
01 March 2025

54567991R00126